D

LIVING IN INDIANA

By

JOY MUCHMORE LACEY

Illustrations by
GEORGE JO MESS

WHEELER PUBLISHING COMPANY
CHICAGO, ILLINOIS

LIVING IN INDIANA

Table of Contents

PART ONE — LIVING IN INDIANA LONG AGO

PART TWO — LIVING IN INDIANA TODAY

*DIRECTIONS FOR USING THE BOOK

To the Teacher
Selected Books for Children and Teachers
Places to Write for Materials
Directed Activities
Suggested Approaches

___

* See pages 118-123.

A Look Through Your New Book

Look at the Table of Contents.

1. How many parts in your book?

2. How many stories in Part One?

3. How many stories in Part Two?

Look at the Pictures and Maps.

1. Does the picture on page 1 tell about living in Indiana today or long ago?

2. What does the map on page 11 show?

3. What does the picture on page 58 tell?

Look at the Book List, the Activities, and Places to Write for Materials on page 119.

1. What is the title of the book you may want to read?

2. What are two activities you may want to carry out?

3. What is one place to write for materials?

Living in Indiana Long Ago

Long years ago no white people lived in Indiana. The land was covered with great forests. Vines and bushes grew thick on the ground. Thousands of buffalo and deer tramped through the forests. Paths were made through the vines and bushes to the rivers. Many tribes of Indians hunted and fished in the forests, rivers, and lakes.

After Columbus discovered America white men explored the great wilderness in the Middle West. That was the beginning of the Indiana you know today.

French explorers and fur traders came first. Years later English-speaking settlers came on flatboats down the Ohio River and in covered wagons across the mountains. Pioneer days in Indiana were full of hardships and danger.

Part One of this book tells the story of early ways of living long years ago in Indiana.

1. White Men Visit Indiana

A canoe, paddled by a tall Indian, moved slowly up the St. Joseph River one December day in 1679. In the canoe sat the young Frenchman, Robert La Salle. He was watching the riverbank. Speaking in the Indian's language, the Frenchman said to the red man, "Pull to the bank. The path we are looking for must be near here."

As the canoe touched the bank La Salle sprang out. Turning quickly he looked down the river where the seven canoes of his party were coming into sight. He waved to the men in the canoes to pull to the water's edge. A stern-faced man, who had but one hand, stepped out of the first canoe to reach the bank. In place of the

1

missing hand he wore one made of iron.

"Have you seen the path, Tonty?" La Salle asked this man.

"Not a sign of it," Tonty answered.

"This must be the place," La Salle replied. "Our Indian guide said that we would find a path leading from the St. Joseph to the Kankakee River. He said that the path would begin where the St. Joseph made its great bend toward the south. We are at that bend now."

"I should not have let our guide go hunting today," Tonty said.

"A venison roast will be most welcome, Ironhand," laughed La Salle, "and surely we can find the path ourselves."

While the men talked, the other canoes pulled up to the bank. Indians,

French priests, and French explorers stepped out. The little company of thirty-two men gathered around La Salle, their leader. Turning to them La Salle gave orders. "You shall make camp and wait here for me," he said. "I am going to search for the path that leads to the Kankakee."

Shouldering his gun Robert La Salle set off through the woods. He watched the ground for the path, or portage, that would lead to the Kankakee River. An hour of walking brought him to the edge of the woods. Before him stretched a swamp. "I can't cross that swamp," La Salle said to himself. "I'll have to make a wide swing around it."

Turning, he followed the edge of the swamp. Daylight began to fade. "It's almost dark," La Salle thought. "I must hurry or night will catch me in the woods."

The Frenchman plunged ahead more quickly, but the swamp stretched on and on. Darkness came. La Salle could no longer see well enough to keep his directions. At last he paused. "I am lost," he said to himself. "But, if I can find my way to the riverbank, I can follow that back to camp."

La Salle stood for a few minutes thinking of the course he had taken. Then he set off again. An hour's walk brought him to the bank of the St. Joseph River. He headed toward the camp. But he had gone only a short distance when he came upon a small campfire. A bed of dry grass was beside the fire.

La Salle stopped short in his tracks. "I must have frightened an Indian away from his bed and campfire," he thought. "But he need not be frightened. I would not harm him." Lifting his voice the Frenchman shouted in an Indian language, "Come back. I will not harm you." But no shout answered his, and no Indian returned to the campfire. One after another La Salle tried all the Indian languages he knew, but still no Indian appeared.

"Well, if he does not want to use this bed, I do," La Salle said to himself. He put more wood on the fire and lay down on the bed of grass. He was soon asleep.

When La Salle awoke the next morning, he was surprised to find his hands blackened by smoke from his fire. Wiping a finger across his face he discovered that it, too, was covered with smoke.

Walking along the riverbank, La Salle saw two opossums hanging by their tails from the limb of a tree. "We'll need furs for extra clothing and covers before the winter is over,"

he thought. He killed the two animals and tied them by their tails to his belt.

"My men will surely be amazed to see a black man decorated with two opossums," La Salle chuckled.

In the early afternoon the Frenchman came into sight of his own camp. He saw his men sitting in a circle around the campfire. They looked worried.

"Hello," La Salle called, stepping out of the shadow of the woods.

The men sprang to their feet and started running toward their leader. "Hello," called Tonty. "Where have you been?" Then, stopping in surprise at La Salle's blackened face and hands, he added, "What has happened to you?"

"Nothing worse than being lost and

blackened with smoke from my camp-fire," laughed La Salle.

"We were worried about you," Tonty said. "When you did not return we searched the woods and fired our guns. But we could not find any sign of you. Come," he added, "you must be tired and hungry. Sit here by the fire and we shall soon have a piece of venison cooked for you."

"Venison!" exclaimed La Salle. "Then the guide must be back from his hunting trip. Now we shall find the path."

"Yes, the guide returned this morning. He is now searching for the path to the Kankakee," Tonty replied.

While Tonty cooked venison, La Salle told the men of his adventure in the woods. Finishing his story, he gladly accepted the venison that Tonty offered him.

"This is good meat, Ironhand," he said. "I hope our guide is as good a pathfinder as he is a hunter."

"Here he comes now!" Tonty exclaimed.

An Indian came out of the woods. With quick, light steps he advanced to the campfire. "Me search long time for path," he said to La Salle. "Many bushes grow over it. But at last me find path."

"That is good," the leader replied.

"Tomorrow we shall continue our journey."

"Winter is upon us," said a priest. "Is it wise for us to continue our journey now?"

"We have traveled the length of Lake Michigan," La Salle replied. "We found the mouth of the St. Joseph River and built a fort there. We have pushed up the St. Joseph River to this spot. Now we must find a portage that leads to the Kankakee River. When we reach that stream we can float down to the Illinois River. The Illinois will carry us to the great Mississippi. Frenchmen have already settled along the St. Lawrence River and explored around the Great Lakes. Some day France must have a chain of forts stretching from the St. Lawrence far down the Mississippi. Only then can we hold this great land for our king."

"The English are settling on the Atlantic Coast," Tonty said. "They are a land-hungry people."

"True," La Salle answered, "but if they will, Frenchmen can control the lakes and rivers of this new land. A few years ago I followed the mighty Ohio River from its headwaters to its falls. Some day, men will float down that great river to settle this new land. France must control the Ohio and all the other waterways."

"That's how we'll beat the land-hungry English," Tonty cried. "We'll build forts and trading posts on all the important lakes and rivers. There are fur-bearing animals in these forests. Fur trade will bring us riches and our traders will help claim this land for France. With forts and trading posts on the waterways we can control the whole land."

"And we'll build churches, too, as well as forts and trading posts," quietly added a priest. "We'll carry the Word of God to the Indians."

The next morning, the Indian guide took them to the portage that led to the Kankakee River. Shouldering their canoes and baggage, the men set out along the path. A five-mile march brought them to a thread of water, barely deep enough to float their canoes.

Setting their canoes into this tiny stream they began their long journey toward the larger rivers to the west.

Gray winter days followed one another as the party floated past swamps and prairies. The hunters found very little game. The men were hungry. Some complained of the hardships and wanted to turn back, but Robert La Salle urged his party on.

"You have traveled country never before visited by white men," the daring young Frenchman said to his men. "You have found a direct way from Lake Michigan to the Mississippi. You go now to build a fort on the Illinois River. It will be one link in the mighty chain of forts by which France will bind her lands along the St. Lawrence to her lands along the Mississippi. Frenchmen, your task lies before you!"

The Beginning of Our State of Indiana

The story of La Salle and his friends is the story of the beginning of our State of Indiana. La Salle and his party were the first white men to visit and explore the land which became our state. It was many years later that white settlers came to live on the land. They gave it the name, **Indiana,** which means, "land of the Indians."

Finding the Answers

Write the answers to these questions on your paper:

1. Why did La Salle and his party need to find the path, or portage, from the St. Joseph River to the Kankakee River?

2. What happened to La Salle when he went alone in search of the path?

3. Who helped La Salle find the portage that led to the Kankakee River?

4. Why did France want to build a chain of forts along the waterways it explored?

5. What kind of man was La Salle? Which words tell the kind of man he was?

weak	French	brave	American
bold	young	old	daring
friendly	cheerful	afraid	watchful

Learning New Words

Match the words and their meanings. Write the new words with their meanings:

1. venison_____   deer meat
2. company_____   hard-faced
3. stern-faced_____   an overland path from one river to another
4. portage_____   low wet land
5. swamp_____   wanting to own land
6. downstream_____   a row of forts
7. land-hungry_____   a place to buy and sell furs
8. explorer_____   a group of men
9. chain of forts_____ grassy land with few or no trees
10. trading post_____   going the way the water is flowing
11. prairie_____   a man who travels to new lands and places
12. headwaters_____   where a river begins

Remembering Names and Places

Find the names in the story that belong in these sentences. Copy the sentences, filling the blanks with the names:

1. Robert La Salle was a_____.
2. Tonty was often called____because he had one iron hand.
3. The guide who found the portage for La Salle was an____.
4. The party planned to float down the Kankakee to the ____ River.
5. France planned to have a chain of forts along the St. Lawrence River and the _____ River.

2. Indiana and the World in Which We Live

You have just read the story of the first white men to visit Indiana, the state in which you live. Many other stories in this book tell about the Indians, the fur traders, the pioneer settlers, and the people who live in Indiana today.

But you will understand these stories better, if we stop here long enough to find from maps what we can about Indiana, the United States, and the world in which we live.

The best map of the world is the globe. It is ball-shaped because the world in which we live is shaped like a ball.

Great bodies of water and land cover the world. On a map the water is usually colored blue. The large bodies of water are called oceans. On the globe in your classroom find these oceans:

1. The Atlantic Ocean
2. The Pacific Ocean
3. The Arctic Ocean
4. The Indian Ocean
5. The Antarctic Ocean

The large bodies of land are called continents. On the globe in your classroom find these continents:

1. Asia
2. Europe
3. Africa
4. Australia
5. North America
6. South America

Many flat maps of the world have been made because they are easier to use. They can be rolled and hung on the wall. They can be folded away in a case. Small maps can be put into books.

On a wall map of the world or on a map in your book find the continents and oceans.

Small bodies of land that are entirely surrounded by water are called islands. On the map find these islands:

Greenland
Cuba

Islands of Japan
British Isles

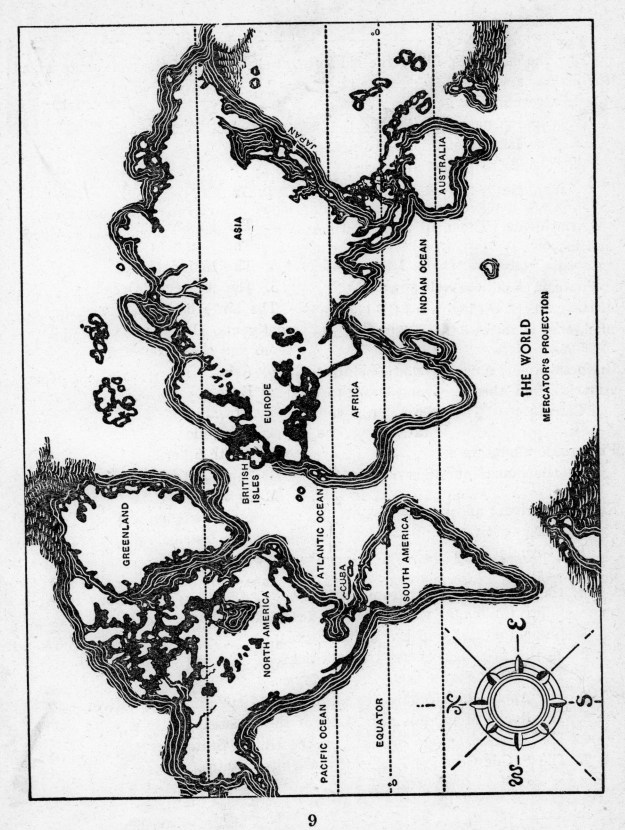

THE WORLD

MERCATOR'S PROJECTION

ASIA

JAPAN

AUSTRALIA

INDIAN OCEAN

EUROPE

AFRICA

BRITISH ISLES

GREENLAND

ATLANTIC OCEAN

CUBA

SOUTH AMERICA

NORTH AMERICA

PACIFIC OCEAN

EQUATOR

9

Copy the sentences, filling the blanks with the names of the continents which the islands are near:

1. Greenland is near _____.
2. Cuba is near _____.
3. The Islands of Japan are near _____.
4. The British Isles are near _____.

There are many sizes and kinds of flat maps. There are maps for each of the continents. The map of a continent can show countries, mountains, rivers, and lakes.

You can tell directions on a map, too. On most maps, north is toward the top of the map. South is toward the bottom of the map. When you stand facing the map, east is toward the right-hand side. West is toward the left-hand side.

North America is the continent on which you live. On the map of North America find these countries:

Canada   The United States   Mexico

Find these mountains:

Appalachian Mountains   Rocky Mountains

Find these rivers and lakes:

Mississippi River   St. Lawrence River
Rio Grande River   The Five Great Lakes

Find the directions—north, south, east, and west, on the map. Copy the sentences, filling the blanks with the right direction words:

1. Canada is _____ of the United States.
2. Mexico is _____ of the United States.
3. The United States is _____ of Mexico.
4. The Appalachian Mountains are _____ of the Mississippi River.
5. The Rocky Mountains are _____ of the Mississippi River.
6. The Atlantic Ocean is _____ of the United States.
7. The Pacific Ocean is _____ of the United States.

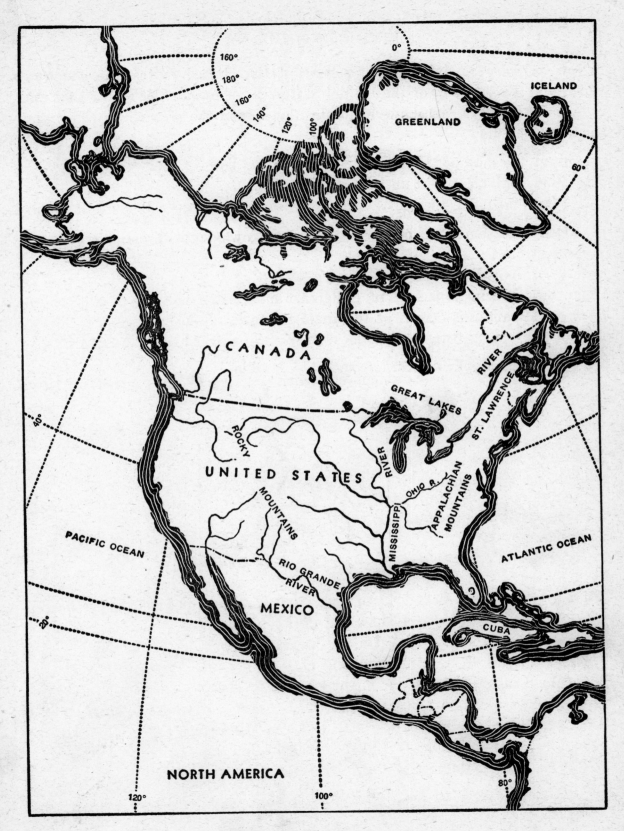

ICELAND

GREENLAND

160°
180°
160°
140°
120°
100°
0°
60°

CANADA

40°

GREAT LAKES

ST. LAWRENCE
RIVER

ROCKY

UNITED STATES

MISSISSIPPI RIVER

OHIO R.

APPALACHIAN
MOUNTAINS

MOUNTAINS

PACIFIC OCEAN

ATLANTIC OCEAN

RIO GRANDE
RIVER

20°

MEXICO

CUBA

NORTH AMERICA

120°
100°
80°

Now you are ready to study a map of the United States, the country in which you live. A map of the United States can show all the states that make up our country. It can show mountains, lakes, and the rivers into which many small streams flow.

Look at the map of the United States in your book.

1. Find Indiana, the state in which you live.
2. Find and name the states that are east, west, north, and south of Indiana.

Copy the sentences, filling the blanks with the right direction word:

    Ohio is _____ of Indiana.

    Illinois is _____ of Indiana.

    Kentucky is _____ of Indiana.

    Michigan is _____ of Indiana.

3. Locate these rivers:

    Mississippi   St. Lawrence   Ohio

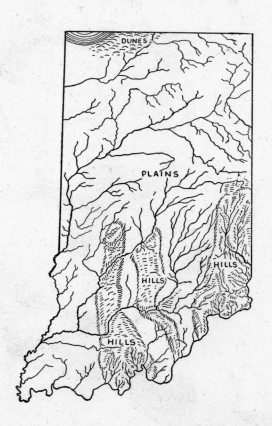

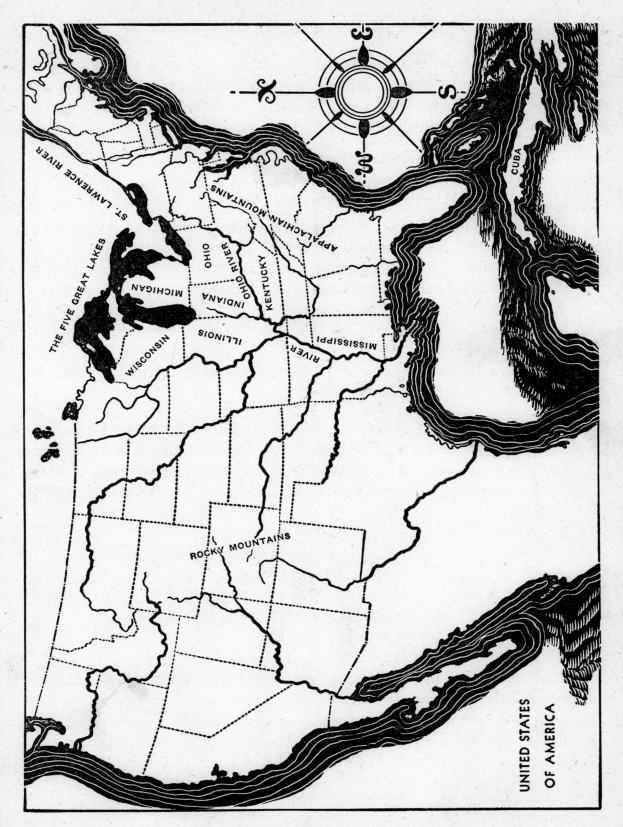

UNITED STATES OF AMERICA

CUBA

ST. LAWRENCE RIVER

THE FIVE GREAT LAKES

APPALACHIAN MOUNTAINS

WISCONSIN

MICHIGAN

ILLINOIS

INDIANA

OHIO

OHIO RIVER

KENTUCKY

MISSISSIPPI

RIVER

ROCKY MOUNTAINS

The map of Indiana, the state in which you live, shows a still smaller part of the world. It shows the 92 counties into which the state is divided. It shows some large cities and the larger rivers and streams in Indiana. The place where a river flows into another river or into some other body of water is called its mouth.

Look at the map of Indiana in your book, on the opposite page.
1. Find the Wabash River.
2. Find the White River with its East Fork and West Fork. Why do you think these two streams are called Forks?
3. Find the Ohio River which makes the southern boundary, or edge, of Indiana.
4. Find Lake Michigan which makes a part of the northern boundary of Indiana.
5. Find Indianapolis, the capital city, almost in the center of the state.
6. Find five other cities.
7. Can you find on a large map of Indiana the county in which you live? Find it on the map in your book.

In the northern part of Indiana are the two small rivers which La Salle and his men explored. Find the St. Joseph River up which they went in their canoes.
1. Find the south bend of the river where they searched for a portage.
2. Show the portage, or path, from the St. Joseph River to the Kankakee River.

Learning New Words

Find the word in the lesson about maps that will complete each of the sentences. Copy the sentences, filling the blanks with the words:
1. A very large body of water is an _____.
2. A very large body of land is a _____.
3. Small bodies of land that are surrounded by water are called _____.
4. Small bodies of water are called _____.
5. A large stream of water into which small streams flow is called a _____.
6. The place where a river flows into another body of water is called its _____.
7. The place where a river begins is called its _____.

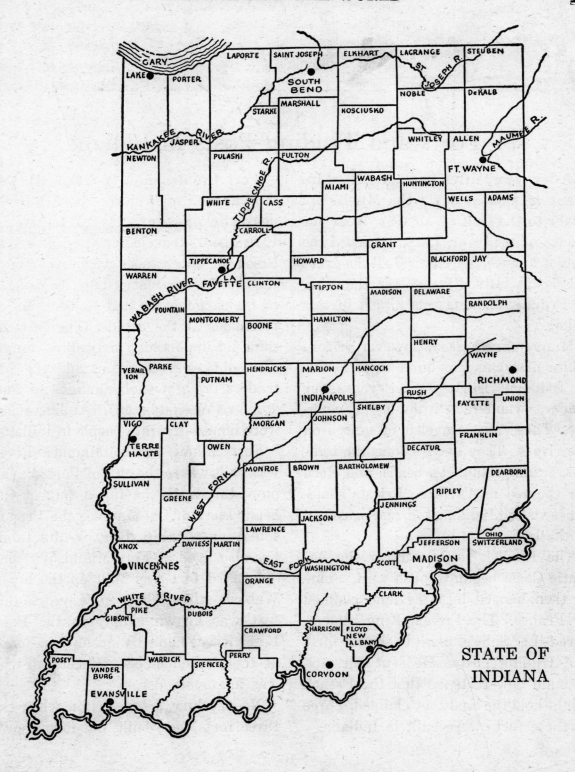

STATE OF
INDIANA

3. Forts and Trading Posts in Indiana

A few years after La Salle visited Indiana he floated down the Mississippi River to the Gulf of Mexico. Near the mouth of the river, La Salle raised the flag of France. He claimed all the great Mississippi River Valley for the King of France. Indiana was a part of this valley.

Many years passed, however, before white men came to build their homes in Indiana. During those years fur traders wandered through the country. These men traveled in canoes on the rivers. They lived among the Indians, trading blankets, beads, and cloth for the red men's furs. Priests sometimes visited Indiana, too, and preached to the Indians.

The English settlers along the Atlantic Coast began to push west. Some of them moved into the land claimed by France. The French King remembered La Salle's plan to build forts and trading posts. He sent out men to build new forts, so that the French might hold the land they claimed. Three of these forts were built in Indiana.

Fort Ouiatenon (Wé-á-ta-non) was built at the rapids on the Wabash River near the present city of Lafayette. Large boats traveled on the lower Wabash, but only canoes were used above the rapids. Furs carried up the Wabash in the large boats had to be changed to canoes at the rapids. The fort became an important fur-trading center. The soldiers at the fort and the fur traders brought their families to Ouiatenon (We-a-ta-non). At last there were homes of white people in Indiana.

Fort Miami on the Maumee River was built where the city of Fort Wayne now stands. By having a fort at the headwaters of the Maumee the French could control this river. White families also lived at Fort Miami.

A third fort was built on the lower Wabash River. For some years this fort was known simply as the Post. Later it was named Vincennes in honor of the French officer, Vincennes, who was in command.

No one knows for certain when the three forts were built, but it is known that there was a fort at Vincennes in 1732. The forts may have been built some years before 1732.

In later years Fort Ouiatenon (We-a-ta-non) and Fort Miami were destroyed. But Post Vincennes continued to be important for many years. A trading post and a town grew up around the fort.

The soldiers in the forts in Indiana helped to protect the French settlers from Indian attacks. They aided the fur traders who sent thousands of skins to France each year. The claims of the French to the Mississippi Valley were made stronger because of the forts. But they could not turn back the English who wished to make this valley their own.

In 1736, Louis St. Ange (Ann) was placed in command of Post Vincennes. When he arrived at the little village on the Wabash he found a group of happy, carefree people. They were French soldiers, farmers, and fur traders.

Near the village was a pasture where all the cows grazed. Near by was a very large field in which each farmer planted his crops. One warm spring day, soon after he came to the post, St. Ange rode out to this field. The farmers were busy with their plowing. Each man used a wooden plow drawn by oxen.

"What will you plant this spring?" St. Ange asked a farmer.

"Corn, to feed my hogs and cattle, and tobacco for my pipe," the man answered. "But I have wheat growing, too. It is wheat that gives us flour for our bread, and flour to ship down the river."

"Do you send many products to market?" the officer asked.

"Yes," the farmer answered cheerfully, "when the boats set out for New Orleans I usually ship flour, pork, and leather."

"Then you are able to buy some goods, too," St. Ange continued.

"Yes," laughed the Frenchman, "a dress for my wife, sugar to please the little ones, and a sharp hoe to use in my field. These and other things, too, I get when I send my products to market."

Riding back toward the fort, St. Ange saw men and women busy at other tasks. The miller was grinding flour, as the windmill turned round and round. A group of women were washing clothes on the riverbank. They spread their clothes on flat stones, beat them with paddles, and dipped them into the river. A housewife was carrying a great pan of bread to the bake oven in her back yard. A hunter walked toward his house carrying prairie chickens and a wild turkey that he had shot.

"There are signs of spring on every hand," St. Ange said to himself, riding on down the village street. Women were digging and planting in the little gardens, their full skirts blowing in the breeze. One old woman had brought her work outdoors. She sat warming herself in the spring sunshine as she braided a straw hat. An old man was whitewashing his log house, while his wife cleaned the inside. The furnishings for the four rooms of the house were piled on the front porch. There were homemade tables, chairs, and beds. There were pictures of the saints for the walls and Indian mats for the floors. A silver teapot and several china cups and saucers from the old home in France stood on a table. Huge feather beds were airing on benches.

St. Ange stopped before the house. "Everyone is busy today," he called to the old man. "You are great workers here at the Post."

The old man laid aside his pipe and looked at the young officer. "Don't be fooled by what you see today," he laughed. "We work hard some days, but we know how to be gay, too. There are dancing, singing, and feasting on all the holidays. We sometimes celebrate a wedding for two or three days. In the summer we row on the river. In the winter we visit, play games, and tell stories. When the harvest is in we have a great feast. In the early spring we have a merrymaking that lasts for several days."

"We Frenchmen are all alike, everywhere," St. Ange smiled. "We know how to work, but we also know how to be merry."

"That is right," the old man agreed. "And we also love our church. Every Sunday we dress in our best, and ride to church in our two-wheeled carts."

The years passed peacefully in the little post on the Wabash. Louis St. Ange was a wise man. Under his command the village grew larger. Farmers sent more products to market. The fur traders had more fur packs. The Indians were friendly. But in other parts of North America, Englishmen, and Frenchmen fought a bitter war for many years.

A fur trader, named Francis Vigo, came to Vincennes one day. "What news do you have of the war?" St. Ange asked.

"The English are winning the victories," the fur trader replied.

"That is bad news." St. Anges shook his head. "If the English win this war, I fear that France may lose her lands."

"The English are a land-hungry peo-

"I have been in command here at Post Vincennes for more than twenty-five years," St. Ange said. "It will be a sad day for me, if I must see the English flag fly where the French flag has floated for so long."

England won the war against France. In 1763 all the land held by France east of the Mississippi River passed into the hands of the English. Indiana was a part of this land.

Post Vincennes was now an English fort. St. Ange's long, useful command was ended. Sadly he left the little post. But he was glad that he did not have to stay to turn the fort over to the English.

ple," Vigo said. "You may be sure they will take this rich Mississippi Valley if they can."

Giving a Play

You can make a good play about the way people lived at Post Vincennes. Plan the scenes. Choose the characters. Think what each character might say. Plan scene three. Scenes 1 and 2 will help you.

Scene 1. Spring planting in the fields near Post Vincennes
Characters: St. Ange and the farmers
Tell what the farmers planted. Tell how the products were traded for things the family needed.

Scene 2. Homework at the Fort
Characters: St. Ange, the miller, the hunter, and the women who were working
Tell how the women were taking care of their homes.
Let the miller, the hunter, and others tell about their work.

Scene 3. ---

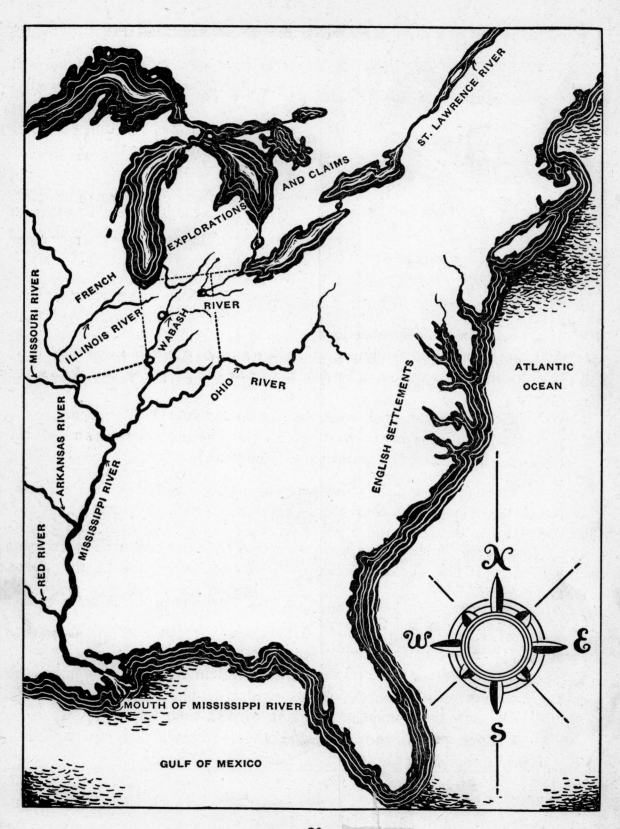

MISSOURI RIVER

FRENCH

EXPLORATIONS

AND CLAIMS

ST. LAWRENCE RIVER

ILLINOIS RIVER

WABASH

RIVER

OHIO

RIVER

ARKANSAS RIVER

RED RIVER

MISSISSIPPI RIVER

ENGLISH SETTLEMENTS

ATLANTIC

OCEAN

N

W

E

S

MOUTH OF MISSISSIPPI RIVER

GULF OF MEXICO

Learning New Words

Match the words and their meanings. Write the new words with their meanings:

1. fort _____   a strong building where soldiers live
2. command _____   a place in a river where the water runs
                                   swiftly
3. settler _____   to give orders and directions to others
4. rapids _____   a leader who gives orders
5. officer _____   a person who comes to live in a new place

Finding the Answers

Write the answers to these questions:

1. Why were forts and trading posts built along the rivers in Indiana?
2. Why did La Salle raise the French flag near the mouth of the Mississippi River?
3. Why did the English push west into the land claimed by the French?
4. When the English won the war against the French, what became of the forts and land along the waterways in the West?

Using the Map

The map on page 20 shows the waterways and the land explored and claimed by the French. It also shows the English settlements along the Atlantic Coast.

1. On the map show the way La Salle reached the Mississippi River and floated down to the Gulf of Mexico.
2. Show where the French flag was raised near the mouth of the Mississippi River.
3. Show where each of the three forts was built in Indiana.
4. Copy the sentences, filling the blanks with the right words from the story:

   Fort Ouiatenon was on the _____ River near what is now _____.

   Fort Miami was on the _____ River near where _____ now stands.

   Post Vincennes was on the _____ River.

4. The Capture of Vincennes

Indiana came under the English flag in 1763. Fourteen years passed, however, before English officers took command of the forts in Indiana. During those years the pleasant, happy life that the settlers had known under the French changed. Because there was no officer in command, men often broke the laws. At all three of the Indiana forts the stockades rotted down, for lack of anyone to keep them in repair. Fur trade was the only business of any importance in Indiana during these years.

Early in 1777, an English officer arrived at Vincennes to take over the command. He built a new stockade and repaired the fort.

The English now had a reason for arming their western posts. In 1775, the Revolutionary War had begun. This war was fought by the English colonies on the Atlantic Coast against England. The people in the colonies called themselves Americans. They wished to be free to form a new nation. A plan was made by the English to stir up the Indians and the French settlers in the West against the Americans. The Indians were willing to join in carrying out the plan, but the French settlers were not. They did not like the English.

One December day in 1777, a tall, sunbrowned, young American colonel named George Rogers Clark, went to see Patrick Henry, governor of Virginia. Virginia was one of the colonies fighting in the Revolutionary War.

"Governor Henry," the young colonel said, "I have a plan that will help the colonies in our war against England."

"Tell me about it," said Governor Henry.

"As you know, the English have a number of forts north of the Ohio River," Clark began. "The officers in command of these forts are arming the Indians. My plan is to seize these forts and gain control of the country north of the Ohio."

"That's a bold plan," Governor Henry replied. "But I must say it's a good one. How can you carry it out?"

"If men and supplies are given to me,

I'll do the rest," young Clark answered. "I have news that the English forts in Illinois and Indiana are not yet strongly armed. A surprise attack would bring these forts under our control."

"It would mean much to our cause to hold this northwestern land," Governor Henry said. "As long as the English control it, Virginia and the other colonies are in danger of attack from that direction."

"It will also mean much to hold the Northwest when the war is over," Clark answered. "When the colonies win their freedom they will form a new nation. That nation will need room to grow toward the west. If we seize the country north of the Ohio now, we can hold it as part of the new nation when the war ends."

"You have a wise head on your young shoulders," laughed the governor. "I suppose Virginia's part will be to furnish the men and the money."

"You are right, sir," Clark replied.

"I must talk the matter over with some other men," the governor said. "But if they feel as I do, I can promise you that Virginia will back you in carrying out your bold plan."

"Thank you, sir," said Clark. "I have spent the last few years on the frontier. But I was born and grew to manhood in Virginia. I shall feel it an honor to serve Virginia, by gaining control of the country north of the Ohio River."

Patrick Henry made good his promise. Colonel George Rogers Clark received money from Virginia to buy supplies. He was given the right to raise men to fight under his command.

In May, 1778, the young leader and his men set out for the Northwest. They traveled in boats down the Ohio River to an island near the falls. Here other men joined the party. Clark trained his men for a time, and then started toward Kaskaskia (Kas-kas'-ki-a), a fort in Illinois. The little company of about one hundred seventy-five men went down the Ohio for some distance. Then hiding their boats they struck off across country toward Kaskaskia. They entered the village at night, surprised the officer in command, and seized control of the fort.

Clark at once sent part of his men to seize other villages and forts in Illinois. These were also taken without any fighting. The French settlers heard for the first time from the Americans that France had promised to help the colonies in their war against England.

The daring young leader had won part of the country north of the Ohio River. But there still remained the English fort at Vincennes. He must find a way to gain control of this fort.

Father Pierre Gibault (Gé-bot) was a French Catholic priest in Kaskaskia. He was friendly to Clark because the colonel had treated the French settlers kindly. One day Clark had a talk with Father Gibault. "Do you know the people in Vincennes, Father?" he asked.

"Yes, Colonel," the priest answered. "I know them very well. I have often visited Vincennes and held services in the church there."

"Do you think the people there would live as well under American rule as they do under the English?" asked Colonel Clark.

"They might live better," Father Gibault replied. "Things have gone badly in Vincennes in recent years."

"Do you know how strong the English are there now?" asked the colonel.

"The fort is not well-defended," the priest answered. "The English officer who was in command is away and there are only a few soldiers at the fort now."

"Would you be willing to go to Vincennes, and explain to the people that they would live better under American rule?" Clark asked.

"Yes," Father Gibault replied. "I will do what you ask. And I shall also be happy to tell my friends in Vincennes that our mother country, France, is now fighting with the Americans."

"You will do a great service to your people by making this trip," Clark said. "I shall send a small party of men with you."

A few days later Father Gibault's party set out for Vincennes. The hot summer days slipped by. Life was quiet and peaceful at Kaskaskia. But George Rogers Clark, waiting for news from Vincennes, was restless and anxious.

Two weeks passed. Then one evening Father Gibault returned to the fort. "I am back with good news," he reported to Clark. "I told the people at Vincennes that our mother country was giving aid to the American cause. The people were eager to accept American rule. They raised an American flag over the fort. One hundred eighty-two citizens promised to be loyal to the American cause."

"This is good news!" shouted George Rogers Clark. "With the Illinois and Indiana forts in our hands, the country north of the Ohio will belong to our new nation."

George Rogers Clark found much to do as the months passed. He dealt firmly with the Indians who threatened to make war on his little force. By his bold manner he kept the red men from attacking him. He sent an officer to take command at Vincennes. A number of French settlers joined his forces. For a time things went well for the Americans. But one January day in 1779, the fur trader, Francis Vigo, arrived at Kaskaskia. He and Clark had already become friends. He brought important news to Clark.

"The English officer, Colonel Henry Hamilton, reached Vincennes last month," Vigo reported. "He captured the fort with very little trouble. He made all the people promise to be loyal to the English. He is repairing the fort. It is his plan to come into Illinois in the spring and once more take this region for the English."

"Then we must strike at once." George Rogers Clark squared his shoulders.

"What will you do, Colonel?" asked Vigo.

"We will march to Vincennes at once and capture the fort from Hamilton," Clark answered.

"It will be a terrible march in the dead of winter," the fur trader said. "Vincennes is two hundred forty miles from here. Heavy rains have flooded much of the ground that you must cross."

"Yes, it will be a hard trip," the colonel admitted. "But we'll march just the same. One thing only disturbs me."

"What is that?" Vigo asked.

"The amount of money that Virginia provided for this undertaking is not very great. I may not have enough to buy supplies for my men."

"Do not be disturbed," Vigo answered. "You are my friend. I believe in the cause for which you fight. My fortune is yours, if you need it."

"Thank you, Vigo," Colonel Clark said. "Such kindness as yours gives me new courage. It may be that I shall have to borrow a sum of money from you, but my country will pay you back. That I promise you."

"I beg of you, think no more of the matter," Vigo answered. "The capture of Vincennes must now be your only thought."

On February 6, 1779, Colonel George Rogers Clark and his one hundred thirty men, set out for Vincennes. Rain fell day after day. Their food was mainly the game they could kill. At night the men slept on the rain-soaked ground. The party had a few horses, but most of the men were on foot. They waded through miles and miles of icy water. They built boats and rafts and crossed flooded streams. The men were wet, cold, hungry, and tired, but Clark kept their spirits high. He made jokes about their hardships. Around the campfire he led them in songs.

The little army came at last to the Wabash River which was crossed a few miles below Vincennes. The men marched on through water up to their necks. A chilling rain fell all day. They spent the night on a little hill. They had no food, not a mouthful for anyone. The next day they struggled on a few miles, and again camped for the night. During the night the weather turned colder, freezing the wet clothing of the hungry men.

The morning sun rose bright and clear. Vincennes lay only six miles ahead. But between the town and the camp stretched four miles of water, covered with a thin coating of ice. Colonel Clark spoke to the men, calling upon them for one last effort. Then quickly drawing his sword he waved it high above his head, and plunged into the water. Shouting men followed their daring leader. The stronger helped the weaker. A canoe went along picking up those who could no longer stand. Foot by foot, the men struggled through the last day's march.

Colonel Clark sent a messenger ahead to warn the people of Vincennes to stay in their houses during the fighting. When darkness came he had his men take up positions around the fort. At his order a shot rang out, then another, and another. The fort was under attack by the Americans. The surprised English in the fort answered the fire.

The attack continued through the night and into the next day. At first Colonel Hamilton refused Clark's demand to surrender. But when the English officer saw his men driven from their cannon by the American bullets he knew he could not hold the fort. On February 25, 1779, Colonel Hamilton surrendered and the American flag was again raised over Vincennes.

Clark and his little army of brave men took the land north of the Ohio River from the English. When the Revolutionary War ended, this land became a part of the new nation, the United States of America. Indiana is a part of the land won by Clark for the United States. Bold, young George Rogers Clark is one of the heroes honored by the people of Indiana.

Getting the Main Ideas

Write the answers to these questions:

1. What was Clark's plan to help the colonies in their war against England?
2. What help did Clark receive from Patrick Henry, the governor of Virginia?
3. What are two reasons why the Americans wanted the forts?
4. How did Father Gibault help Clark in taking Fort Vincennes the first time?
5. Why do you think Colonel Hamilton hurried back to the fort at Vincennes?
6. How did Francis Vigo help Clark take Fort Vincennes the second time?
7. What kind of man was Clark? Which words tell the kind of man Clark was?

soldier	farmer	young	old
wise	honest	foolish	brave
leader	timid	strong	friendly
restless	bold	shy	hero

Using a Map

Use the map on page 20. Find the land won by Clark for the United States.

1. Find Fort Kaskaskia and Fort Vincennes.
2. Show Clark's march from Kaskaskia to Vincennes.

Learning New Words

Match words and their meanings. Write the new words with their meanings:

1. stockade _____   a newly settled place close to lands that have not yet been settled

2. frontier _____   a group of English people living in America

3. seize control _____   a high fence made of tree trunks set upright about a fort

4. repair _____   a man chosen to be the leader of his state or territory

5. English colony _____ to mend
6. governor _____   people living in America
7. nation _____   a group of people living in the same country

8. Americans _____   to gain power over others by force

Remembering Facts in the Right Order

Write the answers to these questions, using only one or two words to answer them:

1. What people first lived happily at Post Vincennes?
2. How many years passed before the English officers took command of the Indiana forts?
3. What name did the people along the Atlantic Coast, who wanted to be free from England, take?
4. What American made plans to take the forts in the West?
5. What was the name of the priest who went to Fort Vincennes for Clark?
6. What was one thing the French people at the fort did to show they were under American rule?
7. What was the name of the English officer who returned to Fort Vincennes when he heard the fort had raised the American flag?
8. What kind of march was it from Fort Kaskaskia to Fort Vincennes?
9. What was the month in which Clark made his march and took Fort Vincennes?

Listening to a Story

George Rogers Clark, by Ross Lockridge, and *Hobnailed Boots*, by Jeannette Nolan, are stories of George Rogers Clark. Ask your teacher to read some of them to you.

5. Indiana Grows Toward Statehood

The United States made a plan of government for the country north of the Ohio River. This region was called the Northwest Territory. It included the land that is now in the states of Ohio, Indiana, Illinois, Michigan, and Wisconsin.

Most of the land in the territory still belonged to the Indians. But white settlers were coming in larger numbers each year. They wanted to get land and build homes there. When the Indians saw white people pushing into the country they became angry. Bands of red men roamed about stealing horses, burning houses, and killing settlers. Some of the tribes prepared for war.

Arthur St. Clair, the governor of the territory, tried to make a treaty of peace with the Indians and to buy their land. But the Indians refused to make a treaty. Governor St. Clair then set out with a small army of frontier fighters to overcome the Indians. Most of St. Clair's men had had little or no training for war.

The red men had a very able leader. He was a chief of the Miami tribe named Little Turtle. Little Turtle and certain other war chiefs led their warriors in an attack on St. Clair's forces. The untrained white soldiers were no match for Little Turtle's warriors. St. Clair's army was badly defeated.

General Anthony Wayne, who had served in the Revolutionary War, was then sent to the Northwest Territory to conquer the Indians. General Wayne spent more than a year raising and training an army. During this time the Indians were again asked to make a treaty with the United States. Many of the strongest tribes refused.

When it became clear that the Indians would not make a treaty General Wayne led his army against them. After falling back for a time, the red men decided to fight. Little Turtle and several other able chiefs were in command. Wayne's soldiers charged fiercely, firing at close range. The Indians dropped their guns for tomahawks, but the

Americans met them with bayonets. The sharp and bloody battle ended in a bad defeat for the Indians.

General Wayne followed his victory by building a fort, which was called in his honor, Fort Wayne. It stood at the headwaters of the Maumee River.

Little Turtle was wise enough to know when he was beaten. He told his people that they should make peace with the white men. Other chiefs agreed with him. When General Wayne called a council to meet at Fort Greenville many tribes were represented there.

White men and red men talked together at Fort Greenville for many weeks in the summer of 1795. At last a treaty was signed between the United States and the Indian tribes represented at the council. The Indians agreed to live at peace with the whites. They also agreed to sell certain lands, most of which were in Ohio. White settlers were soon pouring into the territory. They cleared the land and built new homes.

In 1800, the Northwest Territory was divided into Ohio Territory and Indiana Territory. Indiana Territory included the region that is now Indiana, Illinois, Michigan, and Wisconsin. In later years, as other new territories were formed, Indiana Territory became smaller until it included only the land now in the state of Indiana. William Henry Harrison was named governor of Indiana Territory. Vincennes was the capital of the territory.

On a cold January day in 1801, Governor Harrison arrived at Vincennes. The citizens of the town turned out to welcome the tall, broad-shouldered, young governor and his family. Among those who went forward to shake his hand was Francis Vigo.

"I bid you welcome to Vincennes, sir," Vigo said. "And I shall consider it an honor, if you and your family will be my guests. The Vigo home shall be your home as long as you wish to stay."

"You are more than kind," Governor Harrison replied. "I have heard of your service to Vincennes in past years. I shall consider it an honor to be your guest."

When the public welcome was over, Governor Harrison and his family went to the home of Francis Vigo. There they found a table spread for dinner. After the meal was finished the men sat in front of the roaring fire in the great fireplace.

"It is my plan to buy a farm near Vincennes," said Governor Harrison, "and build a house on it."

"There is good land around the town," Vigo answered, "and it will mean much to us to have the governor's house here. We are all happy that Vincennes has been chosen the capital of the territory."

"You have seen many changes here, haven't you?" the governor asked.

"Yes," said Vigo, "I traded in furs here when Vincennes was a French post. I was in and out of the town when it was under English rule. And now that Vincennes is under the American flag I have come to make my home here."

"It is my country's good fortune that you have chosen to live under our flag," Harrison said. "We owe much to you for the help you gave Colonel Clark."

"Colonel Clark is my friend," Vigo said, as he laid a stick of wood on the fire.

"I hope that I may also be counted among your friends," Governor Harrison continued. "I shall need help from you and all the other citizens of the territory. I face many problems here."

"Yes," Vigo said, "there are many problems, but the greatest one will be to find more land in the territory for settlers."

"To get more land for white settlers we must make treaties with the Indians and buy their land," Governor Harrison said.

"That is right," Vigo replied. "You will need to hold many councils with the red men to get their home lands."

The young governor began very soon to make treaties with the Indians. In each of the treaties a tribe agreed to sell some of its land. By 1809, eight treaties had been made, and most of the southern part of the territory had been sold by the Indians. Settlers came into this region in large numbers. Many of them floated down the Ohio River on flatboats. Some crossed the river from Kentucky. The road from the falls of the Ohio River to Vincennes was filled with travelers.

Some of the Indians objected to giving up their lands. They said that their chiefs had no right to make treaties and sell the land to the United States. They were angry and restless when the white settlers came into the territory. Little Turtle told his red brothers that it would be better to live at peace with white men. But the Indians began to listen to new leaders more than to Little Turtle.

Most important of the new leaders were Tecumseh and his brother, who was often called the Prophet. Tecumseh was a war chief of the Shawnee tribe. He wished to unite all the tribes and drive the white men out of the country north of the Ohio River. The Prophet was a powerful speaker. In his speeches he told his people that they should not follow the ways of white men, but should return to the old customs of the Indians. Like his brother he believed that the Indians should join together and gain back the land that had been sold to the whites.

The Indian village where the brothers lived became a meeting place for Indians who were not contented. This village, afterwards called the Prophet's Town, was on the Wabash River at the mouth of the Tippecanoe River. Here the red men listened to the Prophet's speeches and Tecumseh's plans.

Governor Harrison heard of the meeting at the Prophet's Town. One day he sent for his old friend, Francis Vigo.

The governor had bought a farm at the edge of Vincennes and built a beautiful house on it. Here he lived with his family. Among those who came often to the Harrison home was Francis Vigo, who had opened his own home to the governor when the latter arrived in Vincennes.

When Vigo heard that Governor Harrison wished to see him, he went at once to the governor's house. A servant took him to the Council Room where the governor sat writing. Rising and shaking Vigo's hand, he said, "I am glad to see you, Vigo. I need help."

"I am ready to do anything I can for you," Vigo replied, as he took the seat to which the governor led him.

"I hear that Tecumseh and the Prophet are stirring up the Indians against the whites," Governor Harrison said. He sat down at his writing table and added, "I want you to carry a message to them from me."

"I shall be glad to take a message to Tecumseh and the Prophet," Vigo answered. "What do you want me to say to them?"

"Tell them they must stop this talk of driving out the whites," the governor said. "Tell them that we bought the land and that we intend to remain on it. Tell them that white men and red men can live together in peace if they are willing."

"I shall carry your message to Tecumseh and his brother," Vigo promised. "And I'll bring their reply to you."

A few hours later Francis Vigo set off up the Wabash River. He was on his way to the Prophet's Town.

A week later Vigo again walked into the Council Room in the governor's house. "I am ready to report, sir," he said when greetings were over.

"What reply did you receive from Tecumseh and the Prophet?"

"They said that the chiefs had no right to sell the land. They said they believed that white men should leave the land north of the Ohio River."

"Do you think Tecumseh and his brother mean to lead the Indians to fight, in an effort to drive out white settlers?" asked the governor.

"Yes," Vigo replied. "I think they intend to lead the Indians to war."

"Then the citizens of Indiana Territory must be ready to defend their land and homes," the governor said. Bringing his fist down sharply on the table, he added, "And defend them we will!"

Governor Harrison stood firm against the repeated demands of Tecumseh and the Prophet that white men leave Indiana Territory. But he also tried to get the Indians to accept conditions as they were. Again and again he sent messages to them. He received the Prophet who came twice to Vincennes to see him. When Tecumseh arrived for a visit, with a company of warriors, Governor Harrison spent ten days talking with him. And, at a later time, when the Shawnee war chief came again to Vincennes with a much larger party, Harrison received him kindly.

In all his messages and speeches the governor told the Indians that he wished to be their friend. At the same time he warned them of the danger of joining together to fight white settlers for the land. But Tecumseh and the

Prophet would not give up their plan. Instead Tecumseh went south to get southern tribes to join the tribes in Indiana Territory. In the Prophet's Town warriors gathered, the Prophet preached, and the war drums rolled.

In the fall of 1811, an army under the command of Governor Harrison marched out of Vincennes. Moving north the soldiers followed the course of the Wabash River until they came in sight of the Prophet's Town.

A small band of warriors came out to meet the little army. Speaking through a man who knew the Indian language, Governor Harrison said, "Tonight my men will camp beside the Wabash. Tomorrow I will talk to the Prophet. I promise you that my men will not harm you tonight."

The Indians were pleased when they received this promise. Their leader said, "Indians also promise. They not harm white soldiers tonight."

The warriors returned to the Prophet's Town. The soldiers made camp for the night. Governor Harrison placed strong guards on duty. He ordered the men to sleep with their clothes on, their guns loaded, and their bayonets fixed.

Shortly before dawn the next morning, November 7, savage yells split the air. Then came a burst of gunfire as the Indian warriors rushed into the camp. The guards fired upon the Indians. Other soldiers quickly joined in the fighting. Governor Harrison mounted his horse and rode into the midst of the battle, directing his men. Bullets whizzed through the air. Dead and dying men soon covered the battlefield.

While the battle raged the Prophet stood on a little hill near the battlefield. He sang a war song in a loud voice. He called to his warriors, telling them that they would gain an easy victory. He promised them that the bullets of the white men could do them no harm. But in spite of the Prophet's promises, the bullets of the white men killed and wounded many warriors.

The Indians were badly defeated. They quickly scattered. The Prophet ran away to save his own life. Governor

Harrison's soldiers destroyed the deserted town before they set out on the return march to Vincennes.

The Battle of Tippecanoe broke the power of Tecumseh and the Prophet.

The next year, in 1812, the United States and England went to war. Tecumseh and many other Indians in Indiana Territory fought with the English. William Henry Harrison was made a general in the United States Army. He was given the duty of defending the Northwest. A new governor was named for Indiana Territory.

There were many Indian raids and attacks during the years of the war. General Harrison ordered a line of blockhouses built across the territory. People fled to the nearest blockhouse when an attack came, but surprise raids cost many lives. The Indians in turn suffered severe losses. Their fields were burned; their villages were destroyed; many of their leaders were killed. Tecumseh, the bold Shawnee chief, was killed while fighting for the English.

By 1814, the Indians were ready for peace. They asked for a council. General Harrison and another man met them at Fort Greenville and made a treaty with them. The war between the United States and England ended a few months later. Indiana Territory was once more at peace.

As soon as Indian attacks stopped, settlers came again in great numbers to Indiana. By boat on the rivers, by foot, horseback, and wagon along the roads, people poured into the territory. Francis Vigo, watching the stream of new settlers that passed through Vincennes, said to a friend, "We shall soon have enough people here to become a state."

"That is true," the friend replied. "The number of people in Indiana Territory has grown very rapidly."

"We can thank William Henry Harrison for that growth," Francis Vigo said. "It was he who bought the land from the Indians and opened it to white settlement. It was Harrison who broke the power of Tecumseh and the Prophet when they threatened to make war against the white settlers. It was Harrison who defended the territory against both Indians and English during the War of 1812. Yes, Indiana owes a great debt to William Henry Harrison."

Learning New Words

Match the words and phrases with their meanings. Write the new words with their meanings:

1. council _____
2. treaty _____
3. territory _____
4. warrior _____
5. bayonet _____
6. conquer _____
7. public welcome _____
8. blockhouse _____
9. frontier fighter _____

a man who fights in newly settled land

an agreement

a gathering at which people talk together and settle questions

land that belongs to the government and may sometime become a state

to take in war

an Indian fighter

a party for all the people to greet some person

a sharp blade fastened to the end of a rifle

a strong fort with holes from which men can shoot

Finding the Answers

Write the answers to these questions:

1. How did the Indians try to keep the white settlers out of the Northwest Territory?
2. How did the white settlers try to get the land from the Indians?
3. Who were the three American leaders who had to fight the Indians in order to make Indiana a safe place to live?
4. Who were three Indian leaders who fought to keep the land for the red men?
5. What kind of man was William Henry Harrison? Which words tell about him?

governor	general	fighter
honest	afraid	brave
patient	boastful	friendly
shy	fearless	wise

Using a Map

1. Look at the map of Indiana on page 15 to locate the rivers and towns. Then turn to the map on page 20. Locate the headwaters of the Maumee River where General Wayne built a fort.
2. Locate Indiana Territory.
3. Locate Vincennes, the capital.
4. Locate the Prophet's Town on the Wabash River where the Tippecanoe River flows into the Wabash.
5. Show Governor Harrison's march from Vincennes along the Wabash to the camp near the Prophet's Town.

6. Indiana Becomes a State

Boats floated down the Ohio River and tied up along the Indiana shore. Travelers made their slow way by trail and road into the territory. The offices where land was sold did a rushing business. The newspapers were filled with notices of new towns that were being laid out. Indiana was growing. All over the territory men were asking, "How soon can Indiana become a state?"

In the Congress of the United States, young Jonathan Jennings presented the request of Indiana Territory for statehood. Jennings had been elected by the people of the territory to represent them in Congress. His dark eyes sparkled and his cheeks glowed as he told the members of Congress of the growth of Indiana Territory. He presented his case so well that in April, 1816, Congress passed a law which permitted Indiana Territory to prepare for statehood.

The first step was for the citizens to elect representatives who would make a plan of government for the new state. Such a plan of government is called a constitution. In June 1816, forty-three men chosen by the citizens, met at Corydon, a town in southern Indiana. The capital of Indiana Territory had been moved a few years before from Vincennes to Corydon.

Jonathan Jennings came home. He served as president of the meeting that wrote the new constitution.

The June days were warm, and the meeting room was small. Near by was a giant elm tree with branches spreading like a great, green tent. The convention moved from the hot, uncomfortable room to the shade of the tree. Here the members worked on a plan of government for the new state of Indiana. By the end of the month they had finished writing a constitution.

An election day was set in August. At that time a governor, the members of the legislature, and certain other state officers were elected by the voters. The legislature was the body of men who made the laws for the state. Jonathan Jennings was chosen to be the first governor of Indiana.

The newly-elected officers met in Corydon in November. There they took the last steps necessary for statehood. Indiana Territory was then ready to become the state of Indiana. On December 11, 1816, the government of the United States declared Indiana to be the nineteenth state of the Union.

The first problem facing the new state was that of finding land for settlers. The Indians still had a claim to about two-thirds of the land in Indiana. Councils were held with a number of tribes. At these councils the red men sold their lands and agreed to move farther west. The land that was thus secured in Indiana for white settlement was often called the "New Purchase."

As soon as the treaties were made with the Indians, settlers moved north into the "New Purchase." Other settlers came from the eastern states. Men began to talk of the need for a capital near the center of the state. Governor Jennings mentioned the matter in a message to the legislature.

In 1820, ten men were chosen by the legislature to select a place for a new capital. It was agreed that the men should meet in May at a trading post on the West Fork of White River. Governor Jennings, in company with one of the men, set out from Corydon on horseback for the meeting place. They camped out along the way. They had with them a supply of bacon and coffee and carried a tent on a pack horse.

When the men had gathered at the trading post they started out to explore. They visited three or four places, each of which had been suggested as a good location for the new capital. Several of the men liked a spot on the West Fork of White River at the mouth of Fall Creek.

"The soil here is fertile," one man said. "It will yield the settlers rich harvests."

"But they'll never be able to get the crops to market," another man objected. "The roads are few and poor, and this is a long way from the markets."

"You forget that this location is on the White River," the first man replied. "Boats will soon go up and down the White River as they now travel on the Ohio."

A man from the southern part of the state turned to the speaker. "I think," he smiled, "that you forget that the White River is no such stream as our mighty Ohio."

"This is a good place for the capital, whether or not boats can go up and down the White River," another man in the group said. "It is in almost the exact center of Indiana. That is the proper location for a capital."

"You have set forth good reasons for choosing the location at the mouth of Fall Creek," Governor Jennings said. "I suggest that we look once more at the spot."

The men went together and again studied the land at the mouth of the creek. They agreed that this was the best possible location for the new capital of Indiana.

"Gentlemen, I believe you have chosen well," Governor Jennings said, when the matter was settled. "Today there are two houses on this spot. But some day a great city will stand here in the center of our state."

The report of the men who had chosen the location was accepted by the legislature. Surveyors were sent to measure the land and lay out a town. One of these men had helped survey the land when Washington, D. C., the nation's capital, was laid out. That city had been planned with a circle in its center and with streets running out from the circle as spokes run out from the hub of a wheel.

The surveyor decided that the new Indiana city should have a plan somewhat like that of Washington, D. C. He laid off a great circle around a beautiful grove of sugar maple trees. This was the center of the new city. Wide streets extending out from the circle were then surveyed. Giant trees grew where many of the streets were to be, but the surveyor ran his lines straight and true. It would be the business of settlers to cut the trees and clear the streets of stumps.

In the legislature at Corydon the members were trying to name the new city.

"An Indian name would be suitable," one man said. "I propose that we call the city Tecumseh."

"Tecumseh was an enemy of the white men," another member of the legislature cried, "I object to honoring an enemy by naming our capital city for him."

"If not Tecumseh, then there are other Indian names," the first man replied.

Another member was on his feet. "We want no Indian names," he said. "Let us consider another sort of name."

But someone objected to each name that was suggested. When the legislature closed for the day the newly-planned city still had no name.

The next morning a man spoke to the members of the legislature. "Gentlemen," he said, "I move that our new capital city be called Indianapolis."

No one spoke for a moment. Then one member said, "But that is a strange word. What does it mean?"

"It means city of Indiana," the first speaker answered. "And that is surely a fitting name for our capital."

There was a buzz of discussion, but in the end the name Indianapolis was chosen for the new city on the White River.

People moved to the newly-planned city. Each year the settlement grew larger. Lots were sold. Trees were cut, or deadened, by cutting a ring of bark around the trunk. Cabins were built. Brush was cleared. Gardens were planted. A tavern keeper hung out his sign. A schoolteacher, a preacher, and a doctor settled in the neighborhood. A newspaper was printed. The building of a courthouse was begun.

Then in 1825, the government was moved from Corydon to Indianapolis. The furniture used in the old capital at Corydon was sold. The money belonging to the state was locked into strong, wooden boxes. These boxes and others containing papers and records were loaded into wagons. The state printing press was placed in one of the wagons. Two men, who held state offices, were given the task of moving these goods from Corydon to Indianapolis. They hired the man who owned the wagons and horses to go with them as one of the drivers.

Places were found in the wagons for the families and household goods of the two officers. In the autumn the party set out. They traveled over muddy roads. Sometimes they covered only a few miles in a day. The men slept at night beside the wagons, with their guns near them. The women and children found shelter in the cabins of settlers along the way.

Wearily the little party crept over the muddy roads. On the tenth day, one of the drivers suddenly pulled his horses to a stop. The other drivers followed his example. From one of the wagons the first driver brought a number of bells. He tied one of these on the harness of each horse.

"What are you doing?" a little girl asked him.

"I am putting on the bells, so the people of Indianapolis will know we are coming," the wagon driver replied. "We are moving the government of Indiana to the new capital. The people should be out to welcome us."

Mounting his seat, the driver cracked his whip. The other drivers did the same. The horses strained against their collars. The heavy wagons rolled forward. As the little company drove into the settlement the bells jingled merrily. At the sound, women and children ran out of the cabins. Men left their work and rushed into the streets. Within a few minutes all the people in the town were crowding around the wagons. With a mighty shout they welcomed the government of Indiana to the new capital city, Indianapolis.

Reading and Thinking

Copy these sentences, filling the blanks with words from the story:

1. The first step toward Indiana's becoming a state was _____.
2. On election day Jonathan Jennings was chosen _____.
3. Indiana was declared a state on_____.
4. The first problem of the new state was _____.
5. The people who settled Indiana wanted a new _____.
6. The word "Indianapolis" means _____.

Learning New Words

Match each word with its meaning. Write the new words with their meanings:

1. legislature _____   a meeting for a special purpose.
2. elect _____   a group of people chosen by the people to make the laws
3. convention _____   to choose by voting
4. governed _____   the city where the laws of the state are made
5. capital _____   ruled

Remembering Interesting Facts

Write the answers to these questions, using only a few words to answer them:

1. What direction is Corydon from Indianapolis?
2. How long did it take the two men to make the trip in their wagons?
3. What are three things they took to the new capital?
4. Why did the driver tie bells to the horses when they came to Indianapolis?

7. A Famous Pioneer of Indiana

"Hand me the saw, Abe."

"Here it is, Pappy," said seven-year-old Abraham Lincoln, handing the tool to his father.

Tom Lincoln set to work, sawing the poplar log at his feet into lengths suitable for making a raft. Little Abe hopped about, watching his father, and asking questions in a high, excited voice.

"Gee, Pappy, can you make a raft that will float on the big Ohio River, out of those logs?"

"That's what I aim to do," Tom Lincoln replied.

"How are you going to get to the Ohio?" Abe asked.

"You and I will push the raft into the creek yonder," the father said. He pointed to a little stream that flowed past his Kentucky farm. "I'll float it down the creek to Salt River, and from the Salt into the Ohio River."

"Are you going to travel far on the Ohio?" the boy asked.

"Not very far, Abe," Tom answered. "I aim to find us a new home in Indiana. That state is just across the Ohio

River from Kentucky. But I'll float downstream a way before I make a landing on the Indiana shore."

"Do you reckon you can put all our goods on the raft, Pappy?"

"It will hold my carpenter's tools, your mammy's housekeeping things, and some other goods," Tom Lincoln said.

"Gee, Pappy," the boy cried, "I can hardly wait to get started!"

"I guess you'll have to wait a few weeks," Tom laughed. "I'll take the goods across to Indiana first. Then I'll come back and get you, your sister, Sarah, and your mammy."

When the log raft was finished Tom Lincoln loaded it and set out for Indiana. The raft turned over and dumped his goods into the river, but he was able to fish out a part of them. Tom landed in Indiana and left the goods he had saved with a man who promised to take care of them. He set off on foot to find a piece of land.

On Little Pigeon Creek, about sixteen miles from the Ohio River, Tom located land that he liked. He walked around the edges of the piece that he chose, notching the trees with his axe. Then he cut brush and piled it in great heaps. The notched trees and the brush heaps marked the land as having been claimed. Later Tom Lincoln would go to the land office at Vincennes, file his claim there, and pay $2.00 an acre for the land.

Tom Lincoln returned to Kentucky for his family. On a December day in 1816, they set out for their new home in Indiana. A pot and a kettle, blankets, and bundles were loaded on two horses. Nancy Hanks Lincoln and nine-year-old Sarah climbed on one horse. Tom and Abe mounted the other. The pioneers rode away toward the Ohio River. From time to time on the journey Nancy and Tom walked, to rest the horses.

Tom sold the horses when they reached the river. The Lincoln family carrying their pot and kettle, bundles and blankets, crossed the river on a ferryboat. At the landing on the Indiana side Tom borrowed a yoke of oxen and a wagon. He loaded the goods that he had left on the earlier trip, into the wagon. Then the family climbed in and Tom drove away through the deep woods toward Little Pigeon Creek. The going was slow for there was no road. Within an hour the wagon was forced to stop. Tom jumped down and cut a tree that blocked the way. Abe and Sarah hacked and pulled vines that spread a tangle in their path. Nancy helped pile the underbrush that Tom cut when he had finished the tree. When a path had been cleared the Lincolns once more climbed into the wagon and the oxen made their slow way through the forest. Over rocks and stumps, across low places, and up hills they crept, stopping from time to time for Tom to cut trees or brush. At the end of two days they came to the little hill that Tom Lincoln had chosen for their new home.

Winter had come in Indiana. Banks of gray clouds gave promise that snow was near. The Lincolns needed a shelter at once. Everyone set to work to build a "half-faced camp." Two trees stood about fourteen feet apart. Tom Lincoln used these for corner posts of a rude, three-sided cabin. Three walls were built of poles. The chinks between the poles were stuffed with mud and dried grass. Other poles were laid over the top to form a roof. On top of these, brush and dried grass were piled. The fourth side of the shelter was open to the south.

"We'll keep a fire burning along the open side," Tom Lincoln said. "It will warm us and at the same time give Mammy a place to cook."

"I am afraid the wolves will get us, Pappy," Sarah said, coming near her father.

"The fire will protect us from the wolves and other wild animals," her father replied, as he gave Sarah a pat on the shoulder. "Abe and I will have to cut a great deal of wood, for the fire must be kept going day and night. But there is plenty of wood to be had. We are in the middle of a big forest."

Abe and Sarah gathered dry leaves and spread them thickly over the earth floor of the shelter. They piled great heaps of the leaves in the corners for beds. Nancy shook out the blankets and made up the beds. She set about the shelter the few pieces of household goods that she had, and put her pot and kettle beside the fire. The Lincolns were settled in their new home in Indiana.

Through the winter, Tom Lincoln was busy. He chopped logs for the cabin which he hoped to build in the spring. He also hunted. Game furnished most of the food that the family had, while the skins of the animals provided much of their clothing. Tom often returned to the camp with a deer slung across his shoulders. When he killed a bear he skinned the animal and brought back the skin and the choicest cuts of meat.

Opossums, squirrels, rabbits, raccoons, and wild turkey were eaten by the Lincolns. Pigeons flew about in such great numbers that they could be killed any day when they were wanted.

Nancy Hanks Lincoln was busy, too. She not only cooked the game for her family but she dressed the skins, and when these were cured she sewed them into clothing. She made buckskin trousers and hunting shirts and coonskin caps for Abe and his father. She prepared buckskin moccasins for the family. She was happy to have a bearskin to put on each bed, for extra warmth. Other skins were spread on the floor of the shelter.

Abe and Sarah walked a mile each day to the nearest spring and carried back water. The children also helped their father trim the branches from the logs he cut, and pile the brush, as he cleared new land.

When the family sat beside the fire on winter evenings Tom Lincoln sometimes spoke of his hopes for the future.

One night he said, "Indiana is a new state. A poor man has a better chance here than in the states that have been longer settled."

"Do you think Indiana will ever have schools?" asked Nancy. She added, "I want Abe and Sarah to get some learning from books."

door was a hole cut in one wall. But the hole was so low that Tom and Nancy stooped each time they passed in or out of the cabin. The floor was hard, smooth dirt.

"We must have some furniture," Nancy said to her husband.

"Just give me time and I'll make you some," Tom replied. And he was as good as his word. Soon he had built a framework of poles in one corner of the cabin. Upon this Nancy proudly made up their bed. A smaller bed was made in another corner for Sarah. Tom split logs and built a table. He made it with the flat sides of the logs turned up for the table top. Sticks driven into the rounded sides of the logs formed legs. Three-legged stools were made in the same way from short lengths of logs and sticks. Logs split and used with the flat sides up were called puncheons.

But Tom did not spend all his time building a cabin and making furniture. He cleared a few acres of ground and planted corn, pumpkins, beans, and cabbage. When Tom cleared ground he cut the brush, piled it in heaps, and burned it. But the trees were deadened and the crops planted around them. To deaden a tree Tom cut away the bark in a ring all around the trunk. This caused the tree to die. Sometimes, after the tree was dead, it was cut and

"Oh, yes," her husband replied, "soon enough some schoolmaster will come along and set up a school. The young ones may have to walk a few miles, but in time they'll have a chance to read and write and cipher. And that's as much learning as they'll need."

In the spring, Tom began work on the cabin. By late summer it was finished. The cabin was eighteen feet square, with a loft above the lower room. Wooden pegs driven into the log wall made a ladder. Upon this Abe climbed to the loft, where he slept on a pile of leaves. A stick chimney, well plastered with mud, was built at one side of the cabin. A fire burning in the big fireplace furnished heat and light as well. There was no window. The burned, but often Tom continued to plant his crops around the dead tree.

When Tom went hunting he kept a sharp eye for bee trees. Wild bees lived in hollow trees in the forest. When Tom found one of these trees he and Abe visited it and filled Nancy's kettle with honey. This was almost the only sweet food that the Lincolns had.

All during the summer and autumn, Abe and Sarah wandered in the woods searching for wild fruit and nuts. They found crab apples, plums, grapes, strawberries, and blackberries. As these ripened the children picked them. They carried the fruit to the cabin for their mother to prepare for the table. They gathered nuts and stored them in the cabin for cracking on the hearth on winter nights.

When the corn began to harden Nancy broke the grains by pounding them. She put the corn in the hollowed out top of a hard maple stump and pounded it with a stone. From the broken grains she made corncakes which she baked on an iron griddle set over hot coals on the hearth. A supper of crisp corncakes spread with wild honey was a great treat to Abe and Sarah.

Later, when the corn was ripe and hard, Tom carried a bag of it to the mill. The nearest mill was seventeen miles away, on the bank of the Ohio River. Tom walked, with a bag of corn on his shoulder. At the mill he waited his turn for grinding. He paid the miller for the work he was to do by giving him one-fourth of the grain. When the grinding was finished Tom slung the bag of meal across his shoulder and tramped the seventeen miles back to his cabin.

Another year passed. A few other settlers came to live on Little Pigeon Creek. Then in October, 1818, Nancy Hanks Lincoln became very sick. The nearest doctor was thirty-five miles away. Tom and the children did all they could do. The new neighbors helped, too, but after a few days of illness, Nancy died.

Tom Lincoln sawed a log into boards and made them smooth. He fastened the boards together with wooden pegs that Abe whittled with his knife. When the wooden box was finished, the body of Nancy Hanks Lincoln was laid in it. With the help of the neighbors, Tom and the children buried Nancy on a little hill, not far from the cabin. There was no preacher anywhere near to say a prayer or to speak any words over Nancy's grave. But a few weeks later a preacher from Kentucky, who had known Nancy, visited the settlement on Little Pigeon Creek. Tom Lincoln brought Sarah and Abe to stand beside their mother's grave. The neighbors gathered around, and the preacher said a prayer and made a talk to honor Nancy Hanks Lincoln.

For more than a year, Tom and the children lived in the little cabin with no woman to care for their needs. Then one day Tom left for Kentucky. Abe and Sarah were very lonely with their father away, even though a young cousin was living with them. But one morning in December, 1819, they had a surprise. Abe stepped out of the cabin to see a wagon drawn by four horses coming through the woods.

"Sarah, oh Sarah!" he called. "Come here."

Sarah hurried from the cabin, followed by her cousin. The three watched, in wide-eyed surprise, as the wagon drew up before the cabin. Tom Lincoln jumped down from the driver's seat. Close behind him came a rosy-cheeked, strongly-built woman. Out of the back of the wagon, which was piled with household furnishings, tumbled three children. They were about the ages of Abe and Sarah.

"Here's your new mammy," Tom Lincoln called to his son and daughter.

A smile lighted the face of the woman as her eyes met the surprise in the eyes of Abe and Sarah. Quickly she walked toward the two ragged, dirty children, opened her arms, and gathered them close.

"I reckon we'll be good friends," she said a moment later, when she let them go and stood back to look at them. "Your pappy and I were married the other day in Kentucky. I have come to take care of you, and I have brought my three children. Their name is Johnson and yours is Lincoln, but we are all going to be one family now. Come here John and Sarah Elizabeth and Matilda," she called to the three children standing by the wagon, "come and meet your new brother and sister."

Tom Lincoln began at once to unload the wagon. Out of it came treasures such as Abe and Sarah had never seen. When Tom lifted down a walnut bureau Abe stroked its shining surface with his hard, bony hand. A clothes chest, several feather beds, chairs, a loom, blankets, quilts, pans, and skillets were among the goods that came out of the wagon.

Sarah Lincoln heated water, brought homemade soap out of her belongings, and washed Abe and little Sarah.

"Poor child," she sighed, as she combed the tangles from Abe's coarse, black hair, "you do need a mother's care. Just as soon as Tom gets my loom set I'll weave some linsey-woolsey and make a shirt for you and a dress for your sister."

The coming of Sarah Lincoln made a great change in the life of the Lincolns. She cleaned the cabin. She threw away the leaves and skins and put the children to sleep on feather beds with plenty of blankets and quilts to cover them. She made new clothes to take the place of the worn and dirty deerskins. Best of all she got Tom to improve the cabin.

"I want a good puncheon floor," she said to her husband, "and a real door, hung in an opening tall enough to pass through without stooping. I want you to cut a window and cover it with greased paper so we can have some light. The roof needs fixing, too."

"Well, now Sarah," Tom replied, "I guess I can fix up the place a little to please you."

"You are a good carpenter, Tom," Sarah continued. "While you are about it, you might as well make us a good table and some hickory chairs. And since there are so many of us in the family now, a few more stools would also be of use."

Sarah had her way and the Lincolns enjoyed more comfort than they had ever known before.

Tom had been right when he told Nancy that a schoolmaster would soon set up a school. The winter that Abe was nine years old, a man opened a school a few miles from the Lincoln home. Abe and Sarah went to this school.

The school was held in a log cabin, which had a puncheon floor and puncheon seats for the children. A log had been left out on one side of the cabin. The opening, covered with greased paper, served as a window. A puncheon shelf, along one wall, made a desk where the children could practice writing with quill pens. At one end of the cabin was a huge fireplace.

The schoolmaster taught reading, writing, spelling, and simple arithmetic which was called ciphering. All the children studied aloud at the same time. For this reason the school was known as a "blab," or "loud school." The schoolmaster kept strict order. A dunce cap and a bundle of switches were always on his puncheon desk. Any child who broke the rules could expect to wear the cap, or feel the sting of a switch on his legs.

After a few weeks the school closed and it was several years before another opened in the neighborhood. When the word went round that there was to be a school four miles away, Abe Lincoln said, "I want to go."

"You are getting big enough to help

with the work," Tom Lincoln replied. "It's a waste of time for you to go to school, now."

"Tom, if Abe wants to go to school, he should go," Sarah Lincoln said. "Learning is a good thing. The children should get all they can."

The Lincoln and Johnson children attended the school. Abe learned to write so well that he was soon writing all the family letters and sometimes letters for neighbors as well. He learned to spell and very often "spelled down" all the other pupils at the Friday afternoon spelling match. Abe learned to read quickly and easily. He soon read all the books in the little schoolhouse. Sarah Lincoln had brought a few books from Kentucky. Abe read these again and again. Then he borrowed and read all the books in the Little Pigeon Creek settlement. When he was working, Abe carried a book in his pocket and read it whenever he stopped to rest. One day a book that he borrowed from a neighbor got wet. Abe told the neighbor what had happened and worked two days for the man to pay for the book.

A few years later another schoolmaster taught for a little while in the neighborhood. Abe attended this school, too. He was always eager to learn.

Tom Lincoln helped build a church about a mile from his own house. It was a very fine church for a pioneer settlement. The logs in the walls were squared off instead of being used round. The chimney and fireplace were made of brick.

Tom was a member and an officer of this church. The entire Lincoln family attended whenever there was a preacher to hold services. In those days a preacher often rode from one pioneer settlement to another on horseback. He preached in each place that he visited. Sometimes in the summer or autumn several preachers would meet in a grove of trees and preach. People came from miles around and camped, to attend the services. Such a meeting was called a camp meeting.

On Little Pigeon Creek, as in other pioneer settlements, people helped each other with their work and had fun at the same time. When a farmer had to clear a piece of ground he sent out word that he would hold a logrolling. People came from far and wide. The men cut trees, rolled the logs into piles, and burned them. At a houseraising the men helped build a new cabin. Husking bees were popular with young people. Both boys and girls helped husk corn.

When the work was done at any of these gatherings, the fun began. Usually the women spread a dinner under the trees while the men worked. When the feasting was finished there were games or contests or dancing.

The boys liked contests and games in which they tested each other's strength. Abe Lincoln was often the winner in such events. He had grown into a young giant who could run faster, reach farther, and lift more weight than most men. But Abe also added to the fun because he made jokes and told stories well.

Abe and Sarah Lincoln, John, Sarah Elizabeth, and Matilda Johnson took part in all the merrymaking in the Little Pigeon Creek settlement.

When Abe was not needed at home he worked for the neighbors. Sometimes he helped farmers plow and plant their fields. At harvesttime he helped cut the wheat. This was done with a hand tool called a cradle. He cut corn with a corn knife and stacked the corn in shocks.

Farmers who had land to clear often hired Abe to chop trees. He split the logs into rails, puncheons, and firewood.

A little village grew up about a mile and a half from the Lincoln cabin. Abe worked for both the blacksmith and the storekeeper in the village. He enjoyed the time he spent there. Men from all over the neighborhood gathered at the

store and blacksmith shop when their work was finished. Abe kept the men laughing with his jokes.

When he was sixteen, Abe was hired to run a ferryboat across the Ohio River. At the river he saw many sights that he had never seen before. Flatboats floated down the river loaded with the products of the farms along its course. Pork, flour, cornmeal, skins, and dozens of other articles were on their way to market. Other flatboats carried settlers traveling to new homes. A settler's flatboat usually had a little cabin on it, in which his family lived. Beside the cabin were piles of furniture and tools, and pens in which the farm animals were kept.

Abe also saw steamboats on the Ohio

River. They moved proudly along leaving the slower flatboats far behind. Watching the boats come and go turned Abe's thoughts to faraway places.

"I'd like to go down the Ohio River," the boy said to himself. "I'd like to see what lies beyond Indiana."

Abe's wish came true a few years later. A well-to-do farmer, who lived near the Lincolns, hired Abe to go with the farmer's son on a flatboat to New Orleans. The flatboat was loaded with the products of the southern Indiana farms—hams, bacon, flour, meal, and potatoes.

The two boys floated the flatboat down the Ohio into the Mississippi River, and down that stream to New Orleans. They lived on the boat, tying up each night at some landing along the way. One night a band of men came aboard to steal their goods while the boys slept. But the two boys chased them away, with no harm done except a cut that Abe received on his head.

In New Orleans the young lads sold their goods and the flatboat as well. In this city they saw ships from many parts of the world, and heard sailors speak in many languages. They met old rivermen who told them tales of boating on the Mississippi and the Ohio. They wandered about, looking at the streets and buildings. At last they went on board one of the biggest and best of the river steamboats and traveled back to their Indiana homes.

After Abe had seen New Orleans, the village near his home seemed very small to him. More than ever he wanted to see what lay beyond Indiana. Because of this longing Abe listened with eager ears when his father spoke of moving to another state.

"I hear there is good land over in Illinois," Tom Lincoln said. "I think I'll sell the farm here and move there. It's newer country than Indiana. A man has a better chance in new country."

Sarah Elizabeth and Matilda Johnson were both married by this time. Their husbands and their brother, John, decided to go with Tom Lincoln's family to Illinois. The men built a wagon. When it was done they loaded it with furniture, bedding, clothes, pots, and pans. Tom Lincoln yoked four stout oxen to the wagon.

"Climb in," he called to his family. "We are ready to move on to a new frontier."

It was February 15, 1830, when the Lincolns set out. Abe had just had his twenty-first birthday. He was a full-grown man. He had spent fourteen years as a pioneer in Indiana. Those years had taught him many things that were to prove useful to him later.

The story of the Lincoln family in Indiana is the story of hundreds of other pioneer settlers in our state.

You have already heard many stories of pioneer ways of living. Do you remember how the pioneers cut down trees to build their cabins? Do you remember how they hunted for food and made all their own clothes? The stagecoaches, the first trains, and the flatboats on the river were just as interesting to pioneer boys and girls as airplanes, stream-lined trains, and great steamships are to you.

Read these books for more interesting stories of pioneer days in Indiana.
Smiling Hill Farm, by Miriam Mason.
Bears of Blue River, by Charles Major.
Singing Wheels, by Mabel O'Donnell.

Learning New Words

Match these words and their meanings. Write the new words with their meanings:

1. ferryboat _____
2. carpenter's tools _____
3. half-faced camp _____
4. game _____
5. comfort _____
6. linsey-woolsey _____
7. raft _____

tools to build a house

a boat that carries people and animals across a river

wild animals in the forest

strong goods woven from wool and linen

a cabin with only three sides

easy ways of living

logs tied together so they will float on the water

Making Reports

Choose one of these topics for a report to the class. Read other books. Ask an older person to help you.

Learning the Three R's in Pioneer Schools

A Pioneer Schoolteacher

Making Furniture for the Pioneer Home

Helping a New Settler Build His House

Camp Meeting When the Preacher Comes

Making Candles for Winter Evenings

Keeping Milk and Food Cool

Going for the Doctor When Someone Is Sick

Choosing the Right Heading

Write these headings on your paper:

1. How Pioneers Lived
2. How People Live Today

Read the groups of words below. Then write each group of words under the right heading:

Have electric lights.

Rode in stagecoaches.

Walked miles to the store.

Watched flatboats on the river.

Had log schoolhouses.

Rode in automobiles and airplanes.

Ate ice-cream sodas.

Made candles to light their houses.

Went to picture shows.

Spent vacations at the parks.

Had puncheon floors.

Read many books and papers.

Had many paved highways.

Used tractors on the farms.

Wore deerskin coats and hunting shirts.

Were afraid of Indian raids.

Finding Endings for Sentences

Find the two best endings for each sentence. Write the sentence on your paper, using one of the endings:

1. The pioneers used greased paper to cover the windows because

   it let the light in.

   it kept out the cold and rain.

   it was prettier than glass.

2. The pioneers built their cabins near a spring because

   they needed water to drink.

   they could make it into a well.

   they would not have to carry water.

3. The pioneers cut down trees because

   they needed the logs to burn.

   they needed the logs to build the cabin.

   they did not like trees.

4. The men and boys hunted deer and bear because

   they used the skins for clothes.

   they were afraid of the animals.

   they wanted the meat to eat.

8. Indiana Grows and Grows

The southern part of Indiana was settled earlier than the central and northern parts of the state. There were several reasons for this fact. The Ohio River offered the easiest way to reach Indiana. Settlers who came down the Ohio often found homes near the stream. The southern part of Indiana lay near Kentucky and other states that were settled before Indiana. The Indians gave up their claims to the land in southern Indiana earlier than they did to the parts of the state farther north.

Most of the pioneer settlers of southern Indiana came from the states south and east of Indiana. Many, like the Lincoln family, simply crossed the river from Kentucky.

When the New Purchase freed much of the land in central Indiana from the Indians, a new period of settlement began. Many people living in the southern part of the state moved into the central section. Other settlers came from the eastern part of the United States, and some came from Europe.

Some years later, a third period of settlement carried pioneers into northern Indiana. The part of the state first visited by white men was thus the last part to be settled. Again many people living in parts of the state already settled, moved to the new land. Many settlers came from Ohio and other states farther east. More people came from Europe to this part of Indiana than had come to any other region in the state. The pioneers of northern Indiana usually traveled to their new homes in covered wagons. There were by this time some fairly good roads over which the pioneers could travel.

One of the things that Indiana needed most in early days was roads. The old buffalo trails and Indian paths were the first roads. These were marked or blazed by the pioneers who cut notches in trees along the way. Then the paths were widened and made fit for wagon travel.

The government of the United States had a road built to connect the eastern part of the country with the states farther west. This road ran straight across Indiana from east to west, passing through Indianapolis. It was often called the National Road.

Stagecoaches ran over the National Road. They swept along at fifteen miles an hour. The horses were changed every few miles. It was possible to travel over the National Road from Indianapolis to Washington, D. C., in sixty hours, by stagecoach.

The National Road was much used by pioneers traveling to new homes in the West. A settler living along the road could usually see a covered wagon passing at any daylight hour. At night, the campfires of the travelers blazed all along its length. Many of the later pioneers in Indiana came from the East over the National Road.

Another road that was important in the settlement of Indiana was known as the Michigan Road. It was built by the state. It ran north from Madison, by way of Indianapolis to South Bend, and then west to Michigan City. Thousands of pioneers who settled in northern Indiana traveled to their new homes over the Michigan Road.

Farmers raised good crops. But those farmers who did not live near a river had no way to send their products to market. They wanted some means provided for shipping goods.

For a few years the citizens of Indiana were much interested in building canals. These were planned to connect lakes and rivers so that goods could be shipped by water. The Wabash and Erie Canal was planned to connect Lake Erie and the Wabash River. It was built from Lake Erie to Lafayette, Indiana. Other canals were begun in the state, but most of them were never finished.

Canals cost a great deal of money. The labor of many men was required to build them. Before canals had been long in use, railroads were built in Indiana. These offered better and faster ways to ship goods than canals and rivers furnished. After a few years, the increase in railroads put the canals out of business. Shipping by railroad also reduced the amount of shipping done on the rivers.

The building of railroads was an important forward step in Indiana. Products of the farms were carried to market. Goods made in other parts of the country were shipped into Indiana. Mail service was improved. People traveled more easily and quickly than they had ever done before.

The increase in the number of railroads also helped the growth of factories in Indiana. In pioneer times most of the people were farmers. But as the years passed factories began to appear in the villages and towns. At first these factories supplied only the needs of the people living near by. But with railroads, the factories were able to ship their goods to markets farther away. They could also bring the materials they needed to manufacture from a greater distance. Farming continued to be one of the principal occupations in Indiana, but manufacturing also became important in the state.

One of the most important manufacturing regions developed along the shores of Lake Michigan, in the northwestern corner of Indiana. Much shipping to and from this part of the state was done over the lake, though there were also many railroads serving the region.

Indiana has always tried to provide good schools for its children. The "blab school" of Abe Lincoln's boyhood soon gave way to a better kind. The passing years brought many changes.

One of these resulted from the building of hard-surfaced roads. When children could be carried in school buses over good roads, one large school often took the place of several one-room, country schools. In these larger schools children generally had better opportunities to learn.

Indiana has always taken an important part in the affairs of the nation. Many of its sons and daughters have become famous. Among these are a large number of writers. Indiana business men, lawmakers, public speakers, and leaders in many other fields have helped to make the United States a better country. Indiana has sent one president to the White House. He was Benjamin Harrison, a grandson of William Henry Harrison. Since Indiana entered the Union, the United States has fought five wars. The state has sent its share of fighting men to each of these wars, where they have served with courage and honor.

Making An Outline

Find two or three interesting facts for each topic heading. Then you will have an outline to help you remember how rapidly Indiana grew. Re-read the story to find facts for your outline. Write the completed outline on your paper:

1. Reasons why Southern Indiana was settled first
   a. The Ohio River was an easy way to reach Indiana.
   b. Southern Indiana was near other states that were settled.
   c.

2. The Settlers who came to Central Indiana
   a. Some of the settlers came from Europe.
   b.

3. The Settlement of Northern Indiana
   a. People moved from other parts of the state into northern Indiana.
   b.

4. The Need for Good Roads
   a. Buffalo trails and Indian paths were the first roads.
   b.
   c.

5. The Use of Waterways for Travel
   a. Canals connected lakes and rivers so goods could be shipped.
   b. Products were shipped easily on boats to the market.
   c.

6. The Use of Railroads
   a. Farm products were carried to market more quickly on trains.
   b.
   c.

7. The Growth of Factories
   a. Railroads helped factories to grow.
   b. Goods could be shipped to markets far away.
   c.

8. How Indiana Has Helped Make the United States a Better Nation
   a. Many famous writers, business men, and leaders live in Indiana.
   b.

Living in Indiana Today

The years passed. Thousands of people came to live in Indiana. Indiana changed from a wilderness to a great state in the Middle West.

Each part of the state developed its own way of living. Some people liked to live on farms while others moved to the cities. New inventions made life easier and more interesting.

Little towns grew into large cities. No one part of the state took all the factories. No one section of the state was all farm land. Each part of the state had its mills, factories, stores, and farms. Good roads connected the towns and cities with the countryside.

Part Two of this book tells the story of living in Indiana today.

9. A Visitor Comes to Indiana

One summer day, John Sherman watched a big silver plane circle an Indianapolis airport. A few minutes later the plane landed on the smooth runway. Then, slowly it rolled up to the terminal building and stopped. As the passengers stepped out of the plane, John Sherman walked quickly to the gate.

He waved to a passenger and the young man hurried forward. As they shook hands Sherman said, "Welcome to Indiana, Mr. Hall."

"Thank you," the young man replied. He paused and looked about. "So this is the 'Crossroads of America.'"

"That's right," Sherman nodded. "Indiana is almost in the center of our country. Come," he added, "my car is parked near by. We'll drive to my home in Indianapolis. It is only a few miles from the airport."

Tom Hall followed Sherman to the car and in a few minutes they were on the highway. As they rode along they talked of the reasons Tom Hall had come to Indiana.

The week before, the Chamber of Commerce in Indianapolis had received a letter from a group of business men in the East. "We plan to build some new factories," the letter said. "We want to see what Indiana has to offer us. We would like to send Tom Hall to your state. He will study conditions there and make a report to us."

The Chamber of Commerce was delighted to have Tom Hall come. John Sherman, a member of the Chamber of Commerce, was asked to meet the visitor, help plan his trip through Indiana, and take him to all the places he wanted to see.

"I'm glad you have come to visit us," Sherman said. "You will see that Indiana is a good place to build your factories. The many cities in our state and in the neighboring states are good markets in which to sell your products."

"That is important," Tom Hall replied, "but tell me, are these cities within easy reach?"

"Yes, indeed," answered Sherman. "Our state is crossed north, south, east, and west by many railroads, highways, and airways. You can get your goods to these markets within twenty-four hours. That will save you time and money. You will see what a fine place Indiana is for factories and farms, but you will also see what a fine place it is for people to live."

John Sherman took Tom Hall to his home rather than to a crowded hotel. The Sherman family lived in a very comfortable home and liked visitors.

As the two men stepped out of the car, Mary Sherman and the two Sherman children came to meet them.

"Mr. Hall, this is my wife and these are our two children, Mark and Jean," said John Sherman.

"I am very happy to meet you," Tom Hall replied. "It is very kind of you to take me into your home." Then turning to Mark, he said, "I have a boy just about your age. How he would have enjoyed this trip with me!"

That afternoon the two men made a list of the important places and things to see in Indiana. They decided that a trip to Fort Wayne, South Bend, and Gary would take them through good farm lands and many factory towns and cities in the northern part of the state. Another trip through central Indiana to Terre Haute, Vincennes, Bedford, and Bloomington would show them the coal fields, sand and gravel beds, and stone quarries. On this trip they would also see many farms, large forests, and a number of factories. The men decided to spend one day in Indianapolis to see what it had to offer and to visit the State Government buildings. A three-day trip through southern Indiana would complete Tom Hall's study of the state.

As they finished their plans, John Sherman said, "This evening I shall tell you some interesting things about Indiana that you won't be able to see in the short time you are here. Jean and Mark can help me if I forget anything, for the boys and girls of Indiana study their state in school. Jean and Mark have told me many thrilling stories about early days in Indiana."

When the evening meal was over, the family listened to a news broadcast. Then, they sat in the living room looking at maps and talking about Indiana.

"Indiana is a very good state in many ways," said Sherman. "The climate is favorable for growing many different crops and the soil is deep and fertile. There are many valuable farms in all parts of the state.

"There is just enough cold weather to make people welcome the warm spring days. There is a warm growing season in the summer, the right length for corn, wheat, clover, garden vegetables, berries, and fruits. The cool fall days warn people to put in the winter coal, replace the screens with storm windows, and store the fruits and vegetables."

"We watched the birds come back

this spring!" exclaimed Jean. "We saw the trees bud and listened to the frogs. One day, before school was out, we went to the country to see the baby lambs and pigs. I like spring best of all the seasons."

"Not I," said Mark. "Give me the fall when we go to Brown County and get a bushel of apples. I like the walks in the woods when the leaves are red and brown. Sometimes we see a squirrel storing nuts. Last year I got some pumpkins and corn for Hallowe'en."

Tom Hall smiled at the children, and then turned to John Sherman who continued, "There is rainfall all during the year in just the right amount to keep plants growing and to keep the wells and streams supplied with water."

"Are the rivers important in Indiana?" inquired Hall.

"Yes, we have a few rivers that are important. We also have many small streams," answered Sherman. "As you know the Ohio River forms the southern boundary of Indiana. The Wabash River and the White River wander across the central part of the state and drain the land well. They were famous waterways in the early days. Boats are still used on the Ohio River. Bridges over the rivers for trains and cars make travel across the state easy and fast now."

"The part of Indiana that I saw from the airplane, looked very level," said Hall. "Is all Indiana like that?"

"No," said Sherman. "There are really three parts, or regions, in our state. The northern part around Lake Michigan, has great shifting sand dunes. There are some low hills and many beautiful lakes where people spend their summer vacations. We have a cottage by Lake Wawasee, the largest lake in the state. There is much good farm land in the northern part of the state, too, for the swamps have been drained."

"We'll see that part tomorrow, won't we?" asked Hall.

"Yes," replied Sherman. "The central part of the state forms a second region which contains good farm lands and many minerals. Deep under the good clay soil, the people have discovered layers of coal, pools of oil and gas, and beds of sand, gravel, and limestone.

"Then there is the southern part which is called the 'hill country'. The rolling hills and valleys, with stretches of level farm land to the southwest, make this part of the state very beautiful. People say that Switzerland County looks like Switzerland."

"I know why Switzerland County received its name," said Mark. "We heard the story at school. May I tell, Mr. Hall?"

"I'd like very much to hear your story, Mark," Tom Hall said before Sherman could answer.

"John James Dufour came to America from Switzerland," Mark began. "His father raised grapes and fruits, and that is what John James Dufour wanted to do in America.

"He started west to find a new home. As he was floating down the Ohio River on a flatboat he saw the place he wanted. It looked like his father's home in Switzerland. Dufour bought six hundred acres of land and set out grape vines and apple trees. He wrote to his friends in Switzerland and some of them came to live near him.

"The Swiss people liked the beautiful hills that overlooked the Ohio. They were very happy clearing the land, building log cabins, and making their own furniture. They planted apple orchards and grape vines. They called their new home 'Little Switzerland'."

"It is an interesting story," said Hall. "Have many people come from other countries to live in Indiana?"

"Oh, yes," said Sherman. "Wait till you visit some of the cities and factories in the northern part of the state. You will see workers from Scotland, Hungary, Poland, Germany, Italy, England, and many other countries."

Just then Mary Sherman came in with some glasses of lemonade.

"You have had a long trip, Mr. Hall," she said as she handed her guest a glass. "You must be tired."

"Yes, I am," replied Hall. "But I have enjoyed the day. This drink is good and the facts you have told me about Indiana are interesting. It is growing late, however, and I shall say good night."

Jean was almost asleep, but Mark was wide-awake. When the guest had gone to his room, Mark went straight to his father and said, "School is out. Will you take me on some of the trips you are planning? I'd rather do it than go to camp in July."

"Of course we will," replied his father. "We can't take you tomorrow, for we have already made our plans. We are to be guests of the Fort Wayne Chamber of Commerce. But you can go on the next trip. How is that?"

"Gee, that's great!" Mark raced up the stairs to bed, almost too happy to go to sleep.

Using Maps

Indiana—"The Crossroads of America"

Write two reasons why Indiana is called "The Crossroads of America."

Look at the maps of Indiana on page 12 and page 15. Find the three parts or regions. Write four things you would see on a trip to each of these regions:

1. Northern Indiana

2. Central Indiana

3. Southern Indiana

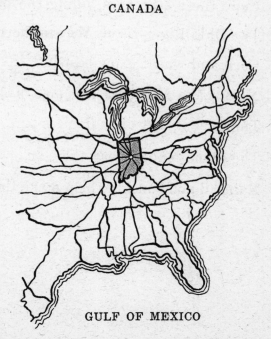

CANADA

GULF OF MEXICO

Answering Questions

1. Write three questions you would ask, if you were a visitor to Indiana for the first time.

2. Write the names of three places you would like to visit.

Learning New Words

Match the words and their meanings. Write the new words with their meanings:

1.	terminal building_____	weather the year round
2.	climate_____	land that grows food crops
3.	fertile soil_____	station at the airport
4.	boundary_____	low hills of loose sand
5.	sand dunes_____	flat
6.	level_____	a line that marks the edge of a place

Copy these sentences, filling the blanks with the new words:

1. The Ohio River forms the southern ____ of Indiana.

2. Corn and wheat grow best in ____ orth

3. Near Lake Michigan are many ____. D.

4. The central part of Indiana is ____.

5. The plane landed near the ____ aptale

6. Rainfall and sunshine help make the ____ of a place.

10. Indiana Weather and Climate

You have just read that Tom Hall wanted to find out about conditions in Indiana, the state in which you live. The rest of the stories tell about a trip through Indiana to find out how people today live, work, and play together in Indiana.

But first, let us learn from maps about the weather and climate of Indiana. Let us find out what we know about our own state.

You know that every day has some kind of weather. There is hot weather and cold weather. There are rainy days, bright days, cool days, hot days, and cloudy days. When we talk about a day at a time, we are talking about weather. But when we talk about all the different kinds of weather we have in a whole year, we use the word climate.

Just as there are many kinds of weather, there are also many kinds of climate. There are cold climates, and hot climates.

A place that has many rainy days has a wet climate.

A place that has many sunny days with little or no rainy weather during the year has a dry climate.

A place that has many cold days and very little warm weather has a cold climate.

A place that has many hot days and very little cool weather has a hot climate.

Then there are places which have neither a hot climate nor a cold climate. The weather in such places changes from day to day so that there are some hot days, some cool days, some cold days, and some warm days. These places have warm, or temperate, climates. The warm climates enjoy the four seasons of the year—spring, summer, fall, and winter.

Can you name a place with a cold climate? A place with a hot climate? A place with a warm climate?

Maps have been made to tell you the kind of climate a country has. As you know, the globe is the best map to study. The globe has been marked to show the parts of the world that have cold climates, hot climates, and warm climates.

The equator is an imaginary line around the world halfway between the north pole and the south pole.

1. Find the north pole and the south pole on a globe. The bodies of land and water near them are very cold. They are covered with snow and ice the whole year around. No trees and few plants grow there.

2. Find the equator on a globe. The bodies of land and water along the equator are very hot. They get the heat from the sun the whole year around.

Other imaginary lines have been made around the world to show how far the cold climates and the hot climates reach. These lines divide the surface of the world into belts which are called zones.

3. Find the zones and the lines that show how wide the belts are on the globe.

Hot, Cold, and Temperate Climates

On the flat map of the world:

1. Find the torrid zone. The torrid zone is the name of the hot belt. The equator is the line that runs through the center of the torrid zone. The climate of the torrid zone is hot.

2. Find the two frigid zones. The frigid zones are the names given to the cold belts around the north pole and the south pole.

3. Find the two temperate zones. The temperate zones are the names given to the warm belts between the torrid zone and the frigid zones.

After you have studied the globe, look at a wall map of the world. You can tell the climate of each continent by the zone in which it lies.

Find the best ending for each sentence. Write the completed sentences on your paper:

1. Nearly all of Asia and Europe are in the
   frigid zone   temperate zone   torrid zone

2. Nearly all of North America is in the
   torrid zone   temperate zone   frigid zone

3. South America is crossed by the
   equator   frigid zone

4. Africa is crossed by the
   equator   frigid zone

If the United States is in the temperate zone, then Indiana is in what zone?

Rainfall and Climate

Rainfall and sunshine have a great deal to do with the climate of a place. Rain and sunshine are needed to make plants grow.

In places where the climate is hot and wet there are many jungles. The rain and sunshine make plants grow very thickly in the jungles. That is why such places are called jungles. People who want to travel through a jungle have to cut paths. There are jungles in South America along the equator.

In places where the climate is hot and dry there are deserts. The land is covered with sand and few trees can grow. There is a desert in the northern part of Africa. There is also a desert in the southwestern part of the United States.

Much of the United States has plenty of rain all during the year. Fruits, vegetables, grains, and trees grow well because the climate is warm and there is much rainfall.

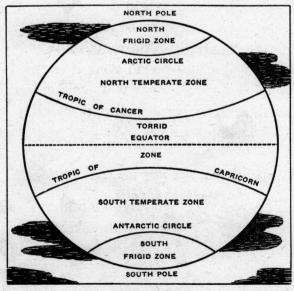

THE WORLD

LIVING IN INDIANA

Now we are ready to find out about the climate of Indiana. Since you live in Indiana, you may know the plants and animals that are found in your state. You know much about the weather and climate, too.

1. Make a list of the fruits and grains that grow well in Indiana.

                Fruits   Grains

2. Make a list of vegetables and flowers that grow in Indiana.

              Vegetables   Flowers

3. Write four things you can do in each of the four seasons.

      Fall   Winter   Spring   Summer

4. Draw some pictures to show games for each season. Let the class guess the season for which your picture is drawn.

5. Find a poem for the season you like best and read it to the class.

6. Keep a weather record for a month. Check the daily weather report in the newspaper with your record.

7. Learn to read the thermometer and keep a temperature record. Ask your teacher to help you.

Learning New Words

Match the words with their meanings. Write the new words with their meanings:

1. torrid zone _____   cold belt
2. frigid zone _____   warm belt
3. temperate zone _____   hot belt
4. equator _____   place farthest north
5. north pole _____   an imaginary line around the middle of the earth
6. south pole _____   place farthest south

11. A Trip Through Northern Indiana

After breakfast Monday morning Tom Hall and John Sherman started on their trip through the northern part of the state. Many of the large industries are located in that region. The car rolled along the smooth highway headed northeast toward Fort Wayne. It ran between level fields of grain, past small farms, and through little towns. Buses, trucks, and many automobiles were coming into Indianapolis. Long freight trains hurried east and west across the state. Several times the men heard airplanes high above them in the sky.

"Years ago, Elwood Haynes drove one of the first automobiles at five miles an hour along a road near this one," said Sherman. "If he were to return today what would he think of the speed and the power of our cars, trains, and airplanes?"

"He would be amazed, I am sure," replied Hall. "Was he an Indiana man?"

"Yes, Elwood Haynes was superintendent of an Indiana gas and oil company when he was a young man," replied Sherman. "Everyday he had to drive many miles to inspect the gas pipelines between cities. The trips were long and tiresome for the horse and for Haynes, too. He began to think about a machine that would take the place of his horse.

"At first he thought a little steam engine or an electric motor would do the work. Then one day he saw a man working on an old gasoline motorboat by the river. He watched the man several minutes. Then he offered to buy the motor. The man was glad to sell it.

"After weeks of hard work Haynes was able to fasten the motor in the front of a light carriage. Two friends helped him pull the carriage, with the motor in it, out into the country where no one could see them.

"Haynes cranked the motor and the three men climbed in. Without a stop, they drove five miles into Kokomo.

"People ran out to see them. Little boys yelled and ran along by the machine. Elwood Haynes was very happy because he had invented a 'horseless carriage'."

"That is all very interesting," said Hall. "What became of Haynes?"

"Elwood Haynes and a friend built one of the first automobile factories in Indiana," replied Sherman. "Very soon they were building several different kinds of 'horseless carriages.' All that was fifty years ago.

"There are many places of interest you will not have time to see," said Sherman. "Southeast of here is Richmond, one of the oldest cities in the state. It was first settled by the soldiers who helped George Rogers Clark capture Fort Vincennes in the early days. Later many Quakers settled in the community. After Richmond was named and a growing city, the Quakers built Earlham College in the town.

"Richmond is quite a railroad center today," continued Sherman. "Famous rose and chrysanthemum greenhouses are located there, too."

As John Sherman finished speaking tall smokestacks could be seen in the distance. The highway passed along the edge of a town.

"Is that Anderson?" Hall asked.

"Yes," Sherman replied. "There are more than fifty large factories in Anderson. Thousands of men are employed in them."

"What is made in the factories?" asked Hall.

"Nearly all of them make something for automobiles," replied Sherman. "One factory makes all kinds of lights for cars—headlights, taillights, fender lights, and dome lights. Another factory makes parts for the motors in automobiles."

They passed through Anderson and soon approached a place with acres of woods and great mounds of earth. Sherman said, "That is Mounds State Park. It is owned by the state. The park offers people in these factory towns a place to rest and have a good time."

"The low, round hills seem to cover the park," said Hall.

"Those are not hills, but great mounds of earth that were built years ago," explained Sherman. "Not much is known about them nor about the people who built them. The mounds were there before the white men came.

"The people who made them were mound-building Indians. Many things have been found buried in the mounds—clay bowls, bows and arrows, heavy clubs, and tools made of copper and flint. Strings of beads and fancy headpieces trimmed with metal snake-heads have been found, too. The mound-building Indians evidently liked farming, hunting, and fishing."

The car sped along several miles while the men enjoyed looking at the farm homes and fields of grain. Then Sherman remarked, "We are now entering Muncie. Muncie grew from a small railroad station into a city with beautiful homes, paved streets, stores, and theaters."

"What made Muncie grow?" asked Hall.

"Muncie has many factories. There are iron mills, rubber factories, and many glass factories. Women who can fruit and vegetables in any part of the United States probably use glass fruit jars made here in Muncie.

"The Ball State Teachers College is located in Muncie, too," added Sherman. "That helped Muncie grow."

"What a good way to see the state and find out what I need to know," said Tom Hall as he made some notes. "You have many interesting stories about Indiana. I shall remember them to tell my son when I get home."

At twelve o'clock the men drove up to the city hall in Fort Wayne. The Mayor, who had his office in the building, was pleased to meet the visitor from the East and was anxious to give him facts about Fort Wayne. He took the two men to a luncheon meeting of the Fort Wayne Chamber of Commerce.

At the luncheon Tom Hall asked many questions about Fort Wayne. He learned that Fort Wayne is a great industrial and railroad center in the heart of rich farm lands. He was told about the railroad yards, the electric company, and the knitting mills. The Mayor explained that there were factories making nearly everything—car wheels, washing machines, radios, tents, boilers, tanks, and trucks. One of the men told Hall that Fort Wayne was named for General Anthony Wayne, a hero of Indian days.

"I would like to stay here for a week," said Hall, as he shook hands with the Mayor, "but we must get to South Bend this afternoon."

For more than sixty miles the men drove by large farms, woodlands, and beautiful lakes. They saw people fishing, swimming, picnicking, and playing games. Then the countryside began to change. The farms, woods, and lakes gave place to little towns, gas stations, eating places, and cities.

"Does your son play in the school band?" asked Sherman.

"Yes, he does," Hall answered. "He plays a cornet."

"That cornet was probably made here in Elkhart," said Sherman driving slowly through the main street of the city. "All sorts of band instruments are made in Elkhart. These instruments are used all over the United States."

The travelers came to Mishawaka

before they realized they had left Elkhart, for the two cities are only a few miles apart.

"Here is where your rubber boots, galoshes, and raincoats are made," laughed Sherman. "In this part of the state we can feed you, outfit you with woolen clothes, rubber shoes, and raincoats, and furnish you with an automobile, a truck, or a plane."

Driving through Mishawaka the men soon entered South Bend.

"This is one of Indiana's largest cities," Sherman said. "It owes much of its growth to men who started small factories years ago. The factories have grown into great industries."

"Who were some of these men?" asked Hall.

"One was John Studebaker. The Studebaker family came to Indiana in a big, covered wagon in the pioneer days. There were five brothers and they were all wagonmakers.

"That was in the early days. John Studebaker often told how their business grew. At first they had workers in one small building and a blacksmith shop. Now the company has thousands of workers in a modern automobile factory. In a museum room, at the factory, is the covered wagon in which the Studebakers came to Indiana. There are also some early wagons and all the different models of automobiles they have made."

"That would be an interesting place to visit, if we had time," said Hall. "What other factories are in South Bend?"

"There are about one hundred fifty factories in South Bend," replied Sherman. "One of the largest factories makes airplane parts and household machines, such as washing machines, fans, and irons. Another very large factory makes all kinds of farm machines and tools. One makes brakes for cars, while another makes gears."

John Sherman drove slowly through the city so that his friend could see the factories.

"Some of the factories look like cities," said Hall.

"You are right," agreed Sherman. "One factory has paved streets, homes for its workers, stores, theaters, and buses of its own. The buildings at this factory cover several acres of land.

The men stopped for the night at a hotel. After dinner Hall said, "I should like to know something about Gary before we get there tomorrow."

"There is a small booklet at the newsstand," said Sherman. "I saw it when I bought my newspaper."

"That is fine," said Hall. "I'll buy one and read it this evening."

Choosing the Right Headings

Write these headings on your paper:

1. Early Indiana   2. Indiana Today

Read the groups of words. Then write each group of words under the right heading:

Many railways and highways

Large cities with factories

Large forests in which deer live

Stagecoaches before the doors of hotels

Well-kept farmyards and homes

Fields of corn, wheat, and clover

Wells and pumps for each family

Buses and street cars in the cities

Forts and trading posts along the rivers

People picnicking in parks

Long freight trains going east and west

Airplanes in the skies

Finding Out About Our Communities

Write the answers to these questions on your paper:

1. What factories are located in your home community?
2. What are some of the products made in the factories?
3. How are the automobiles today different from the early ones? Ask your grandparents to tell you about the first automobiles in which they rode.
4. How are the roads today different from the roads the pioneers traveled?
5. What are some things we have today that make our ways of living easier than were the ways of the pioneers?

Learning About Cities

Look at the map on page 15. Locate the cities named in the story.

1. Write on your paper one or two things made in each of these cities:

Fort Wayne _____   Muncie _____

Mishawaka _____   Anderson _____

Elkhart _____   South Bend _____

2. Write the answers to these questions: How did Fort Wayne get its name? Why do you think South Bend was given its name?

12. Gary, the Steel City of Indiana

While John Sherman read his newspaper, Tom Hall read the story of Gary:

An engineer for a great steel company was walking along the shifting sand dunes in northern Indiana one summer day in 1904. All about him stretched miles of sand. Only a few small oak trees grew in the sand.

Lake Michigan forms part of the boundary of Indiana. The engineer stood on the shore of the lake a long time. He gazed at the sand dunes and then looked out across the blue waters.

"This is a wonderful spot. If I can only make them understand. It will cost very little to buy the land," he said to himself.

In his mind the young engineer planned a new city, a new factory, and new homes for thousands of workers. He looked to the north and imagined that he saw great boats bringing iron ore from the mines around Lake Superior, down Lake Michigan, to the place where he stood. He looked to the south and saw long trains of coal and limestone rushing toward him.

He glanced about him and saw a huge steel mill with smoke rolling from its smokestacks. He saw piles of coal, ovens of coke, and blast furnaces turning iron ore into steel. He saw trains carrying steel products to all parts of the country.

All these things he saw in his mind instead of the sand dunes around Lake Michigan. He turned and walked thoughtfully away.

The next week the president of the steel company called together a group of engineers and business men. He told them the company wished to build a new steel mill larger than any of the mills they had at the time. He asked them to help find a new location close to coal fields, stone quarries, and railroads.

When some of the older men had spoken, the engineer who had visited northern Indiana asked to be heard. He said, "I should like to tell you about a place I saw last week. The miles of sand dunes near Lake Michigan are worthless. Nothing of value will grow in the sand. Part of the land is marshy. Buy both the sandy and the marshy land, for thousands of acres will be needed to build the enormous steel mills you are planning.

"Call in business men, engineers, and surveyors, and plan a new city to be built around the steel mills. If it is well planned the new city will become the steel center of the Middle West. Steel products can be sent by boat or train to all parts of the country."

That was the beginning of Gary, for the steel company liked the plans of the engineer. About ten thousand acres of sand dunes and marshlands along the shore of Lake Michigan were bought. The land was surveyed, cleared, and drained.

Surveyors and engineers worked together. They located a place for the mills on the shores of the lake. They laid many lines of railway tracks to bring in coal and limestone and to carry away the steel products. South of the tracks they laid out a city with wide streets, a business section, and blocks of land for houses, parks, and schools. Blueprints of the buildings were made. A new harbor was built for the heavy boats loaded with iron ore. A new city was planned.

"There is plenty of land," said the surveyors. "The houses can have yards and gardens. The streets will be wide. Good roads leading to other towns will be built."

"A good water system, telephones, and electric lights will be needed in the mills and in the homes," said the engineer. "The city must be a healthful place to live."

One man said, "We want good schools for our children, something new and different from the schools we attended. Let us find a schoolman to plan the school system of Gary."

Other men thought of churches, banks, stores, theaters, hotels, and parks. Each group set to work quickly.

Newspapers all over the United States told people that there was much work for men at Gary and that the pay was good.

The first office of the steel company was an old boxcar. The first homes of the workers were tents and shacks covered with heavy paper. Almost overnight, the sand dunes became a busy, crowded settlement.

In two years many of the tents and shacks had been replaced with houses. As soon as a hundred houses were finished the people bought them and the shacks were torn down. The houses were sold only to people working for the steel company. The mills with their smokestacks and blast furnaces went up rapidly. People came from many other states to help. Whole families came from Poland, Italy, Germany, and other countries. Many Negroes left their homes in the South and found work in the new city.

Fires were started in the mills in 1908. It was a great day for the ten thousand people who lived in Gary. Boats brought in the iron ore. The coal fields in Indiana furnished much coal for the coke ovens. Stores and banks were busy. In the fall, schools opened.

"Not many cities grow as fast as Gary did," said Hall as he looked up from his book. "Will we be able to visit the steel mills there tomorrow?"

"Oh, yes, I have passes that will let us in," Sherman replied. "And if we are to make an early start tomorrow, we should get to bed soon."

After an early breakfast the next morning, the two men started for Gary. They wanted to see the thousands of workers on the "day shift" taking the places of the men who worked on the "night shift."

"When business is good for the mills, people have money to spend for food and clothes, for doctor and dentist bills, and for shows and cars," said Sherman.

"How is business in Gary today?" asked Tom Hall.

"Very good," answered Sherman.

"Steel is needed for so many things."

As the men drew near the mills, they crossed many railroad tracks which separate the mills from the city. Along the lake stretched rows and rows of buildings. The men were just in time to see the workers passing through the gates to and from the mills. They came out on foot, in buses, in automobiles, and in cars that belonged to the mills. Thousands of men went into the mills.

"There seem to be plenty of workers in this part of the state," said Hall. "Mills and factories are like beehives. We have seen thousands of people going to work."

"The men are paid well and they have steady work," said Sherman. Nearly all of them who came from other countries have become American citizens, and their children are real Americans. They like our way of living."

When the shift of workers was finished, the men presented their passes to the gateman. He directed them to the main office building. From there a guide took them to the yards which were filled with piles of iron ore, coal, coke, limestone, and scrap iron. The guide showed them the blast furnaces and explained how the iron was melted from the ore. The visitors walked through the rolling mills where steel bars were rolled into sheets for automobiles, airplanes, ships, and railway cars. The guide told them that the steel was shipped to factories in South Bend, Fort Wayne, Chicago, Detroit, and other cities in many parts of the country.

"Every city seems to have a factory of its own," said Hall.

"Yes, that is one of the interesting things about industries in Indiana," replied Sherman. "Almost every city has some kind of factory for its workers. The larger cities have many different kinds of factories. We have good locations for factories in every part of the state."

"Well, well, I was beginning to think I had found the place right here in northern Indiana," said Hall. "But perhaps you are right. I'll have to see the whole state to get a real idea of what Indiana has to offer."

All morning the men talked, asked questions, and listened to the guide.

Time passed quickly. It was two o'clock before they left. In the afternoon they drove through East Chicago, Whiting, and Hammond where they saw oil refineries, soap factories, and factories that make parts for machines and cars. Each city had its stores, theaters, parks, schools, churches, and hospitals to take care of its people.

Returning to Indianapolis, the men drove through some of the best farm lands of Indiana. The car rolled along the smooth highway past comfortable farm homes, past hundreds of cattle grazing in the pastures, and between acres and acres of planted fields.

At Lafayette, Sherman telephoned Purdue University to invite one of their men to go with them on a trip through one of the farming regions of Indiana the next day.

Purdue University was glad to send James Oliver, one of their men who lived in Indianapolis, to tell the visitor about agriculture in Indiana.

"That is fine. That will be a great help," said Hall when Sherman told him that James Oliver would go with them.

At six o'clock, the car drove up in front of the Sherman home in Indianapolis. Mary Sherman was on the front porch.

"Did you have a nice trip?" she asked. "Are you finding what you want?"

"Indeed, yes," smiled Tom Hall. "It seems more like a vacation trip than a business trip. Yet I am getting just the things the company wants to know."

Questions to Answer

Write the answers to these questions on your paper:

1. If you visited a steel mill, what are some questions you would ask about the making of steel from iron ore?
2. What are some uses of steel? Make a list of the steel products found in or at the following places:

Houses   Schools   Farms

Using a Map

Look at the map of Indiana on page 15.
1. Find Gary on Lake Michigan.
2. Find Hammond, East Chicago, and Whiting on a road map of Indiana.
3. On the map show the roads the men traveled when returning home from Gary. Locate Lafayette where the men stopped for a few minutes.

Learning New Words

Match the words and their meanings. Write the new words with their meanings:

1. harbor _____
2. surveyor _____
3. agriculture _____
4. coke _____
5. stone quarry _____

6. blast furnace _____

7. blueprint _____

8. oil refinery _____
9. enormous _____

a product made by heating coal in an oven

very large

a man who measures land

farming

holes or open places in the ground from which blocks of stone are taken

a furnace where blasts of air make a very hot fire to melt iron ore

a protected place on the shore of the lake for boats

a plan of a building

a place where oil is made pure and changed into other products

13. A Trip Through Central Indiana

"Time to get up, Mark, if you are going with us today. It is six o'clock," called his father on Wednesday morning.

Mark tumbled out of bed and was ready for breakfast in a jiffy. When breakfast was over the two men and Mark put their suitcases in the trunk of the car. Mark had a road map of Indiana. He also had a little book in which he planned to keep the mileage of the trip.

"I'll sit in the back seat," said Hall, as he opened the car door. "That will make it easier for Mr. Oliver, the man from Purdue, to tell me about the land."

Mark and his father climbed into the front seat and the party was off to pick up James Oliver.

"Mr. Oliver can tell you a great deal about agriculture in Indiana," said Sherman. "He is a friend of all the farmers and their families. He knows all the different farm crops and the best stock farms. Perhaps he will show you some of the prize hogs and calves that farmers take to the state fair."

The car stopped before the Oliver home and John Sherman introduced the two men. James Oliver took his place in the car and the party was off on another trip through Indiana. They drove west on Highway 40, the old National Road. Everyone enjoyed looking at the neat well-kept farm homes with their many farm buildings, their gardens, and their small orchards. They stopped now and then to look at a field of waving wheat or to admire the straight rows of green corn. Sometimes they watched a herd of sheep in a pasture or cattle standing near a barn.

"Oh, look at the little black pigs with bands of white around their fat bodies," exclaimed Mark. "Look at them run!"

The little pigs ran and squealed. Some of them hid while others stuck their noses through the fence and tried to get out.

As they drove along, James Oliver explained how Purdue University helps thousands of men, women, boys, and girls to be better farmers. He told about the men from Purdue who go all over the state talking with groups of farmers. Men who have studied farming at Purdue are hired to be county agents. They advise the farmers about seeds, planting, the care of livestock, and other farm problems.

"It must take many men to visit and talk with all the farmers," said Hall. "Isn't there some other way to do it?"

"We do have other ways," replied Oliver. "Each year we invite the farmers to come for two weeks to Purdue University. We have interesting talks and movies about farm life."

"Do many come?" asked Hall.

"Oh, yes," said Oliver. "Hundreds of farmers come. They learn how to drain their land. They see the newest kinds of farm machines and tools. They learn about barns, hog houses, and farm buildings."

Then James Oliver told about the 4-H Clubs. He said that they are the farm clubs for boys and girls directed by the high school teachers of agriculture and home economics. The girls belong to cooking, canning, and sewing clubs. The boys have corn clubs, pig clubs, and calf clubs. Many of the boys and girls win prizes at the county fairs for their club work. During the summer the club members may spend four days at a summer camp in a state park.

"No wonder Purdue is a great University!" Hall exclaimed. "It does much to help farming and make living in the country interesting. But Purdue trains men for other work as well as for farming, doesn't it?"

"Oh, yes," Oliver replied. "It has a school for engineers, and it trains girls, too. They learn about cooking, sewing, and homemaking. Sometimes ten thousand students are on the campus at one time."

"I am interested in the crops you grow in Indiana," Hall said, as he took out his notebook to jot down some facts.

"More corn is raised in Indiana than any other grain, but there is plenty of wheat, oats, and soybeans, too," Oliver said. "Thousands of bushels of onions and potatoes are grown in the rich, black soil in northern Indiana. Near the Michigan-Indiana state line there are great mint farms. In the southern part of the state the farmers grow melons, tomatoes, and fruits. Indiana leads the nation in the growing and the canning of tomatoes."

"I suppose the farmers use many machines," Hall said.

"Yes, they have many machines," replied Oliver. "Nearly all of them have tractors. The tractors are used to pull the plows, seeders, and cultivators."

When Mark heard the word, "plow," he said, "Mr. Oliver, I want to ask you a question. Are you the James Oliver who invented the steel plow for the farmers?"

"Oh, no, but I wish I were," laughed Oliver. "He was my great-grandfather. What do you know about him, young man?"

"We learned about him at school," answered Mark. "He made the first steel plow. Our teacher said that James Oliver came from Scotland."

"Yes," said Oliver. "That is right. There was a large family and all the children had to work hard. John and Andrew Oliver, the two oldest boys, and their sister, Jane, came to America to find work, as soon as they were old enough to leave home.

"In every letter they wrote to their father, they begged him to sell his house and land in Scotland and come to America to live. They told him there was plenty of work and that the pay was good. They told him about the cheap farm land in Indiana. That was a long time ago. At last the Olivers sailed for America."

"Did they come on one of the big boats?" asked Mark.

"Yes," said Mr. Oliver. "John, Andrew, and Jane met them. The family was glad to be together again. They came out west to live near Mishawaka, Indiana. James, a big strong boy, found work in an iron foundry. Do you know what that is, Mark?"

"I think it is a place where iron is made into machines and tools," replied Mark.

"You are right," said Oliver. "James Oliver liked his work. When he was a young man he was able to buy a small iron foundry in South Bend. Part of the foundry was a plow factory, and that was what interested James most.

"He said to himself, 'A steel plow would make farming easier. I'll make a plow that is strong and light. It must cut deep into the soil and turn it over in a straight row. Every farmer will need a plow.' For twelve years he worked on his plan for a steel plow. At last he was ready to get a patent on it."

"What is that?" asked Mark who was listening to every word.

"A patent is a statement from the government," answered Oliver. "The patent said that only James Oliver could make and sell the Oliver Chilled Plow, which was the name of his invention."

"It was a wonderful invention," said Hall. "I suppose he sold many plows."

"Yes, it was a wonderful invention," said Oliver. "Farmers everywhere bought steel plows and James Oliver became a very rich man. Today many people still use Oliver plows."

As he finished the story Oliver

turned to Mark and asked, "Is that the story you learned at school, Mark?"

"It is the very same story," said Mark. "I'm going to see if the name, 'Oliver,' is on any of the plows we see today."

The car sped along past many small farms. Each one had some pigs, chickens, and cows as well as an orchard and a garden. When the party came to Brazil they saw fields of clay used for making brick, tile, sewer pipe, and building blocks.

"There are a dozen clay plants here," explained Oliver. "The tile and sewer pipe are used to drain the land and carry away sewage. The bricks are used for homes and large buildings. The clay industry is a very important one in Indiana."

"Around Brazil are many coal fields, too," said Sherman. "A few miles to the south are large strip mines. We have time to visit them if you wish."

"I'd like to very much," said Hall.

The car turned south on a little side road. "Look at the big steam shovel!" cried Mark. "Let's stop and watch it."

The car was parked by the roadside, and the party walked nearer the strip mine to watch the mighty machine at work. Each time the big arm of the machine swung around in a half circle, it bit into the ground. It slowly scooped tons of dirt to one side and uncovered

a layer of coal. Then a smaller shovel scooped great lumps of coal into trucks that were waiting.

"Sometimes the coal is loaded into railway cars," said Oliver. "A few miles south of here is a deep shaft mine. I think we should see it, too."

"So this is where the Gary steel mills and the railroad yards at Fort Wayne get some of their coal," said Hall as they climbed into the car and started south.

"That is right," said Oliver. "Thousands of tons of coal are shipped to all parts of the state and nation from these mines."

As the party approached the shaft mine they saw the many buildings, railroad tracks, and cars of coal.

"What is the tall tower?" asked Mark.

"That is the tipple from which the elevators are hung," explained Oliver. "The tipple is built over the shafts."

"What are the shafts?" asked Mark.

Then James Oliver explained that every shaft mine has two deep well-like openings into the ground. "These openings are called shafts," said Oliver. "They are the entrances to the mine. The up-shaft and the down-shaft carry air underground to the miners who are working. The elevators travel up and down the shafts just as the elevator cars do in a tall building. They carry the men down to work and bring cars of coal up to the surface. Some of the shaft mines are like underground cities."

"From the piles of coal I see, Indiana seems well supplied," said Hall.

"Yes," replied Oliver as they were leaving. "There is enough coal to last for many years. However, Indiana watches the supply carefully and makes good use of every ton."

The party turned back to Highway 40 and soon arrived in Terre Haute.

"Mark tells me this is the 'Crossroads of Indiana,'" laughed Sherman. "For here Highway 40, the old National Road east and west, crosses Highway 41. This is the main highway north and south from Chicago to Florida."

"What is there to see in Terre Haute?" asked Hall.

"I wish we had time to visit the Dresser Power Plant on the Wabash River, a few miles west of Terre Haute," replied Sherman. "It is a huge plant that furnishes electricity for many parts of Indiana and some of its neighbor states. It has its own coal mine and many men work there. There are many canning factories and food markets here, too."

"Terre Haute has one of the state schools, the Indiana State Teachers College," added Oliver.

A few minutes later the party turned left on Highway 41 and drove south through the city of Terre Haute.

"Oh, look at the glass houses!" cried Mark. "What are they?"

"Those are gardens where all during the year cucumbers and tomatoes grow under glass. Those greenhouses cover thirty-five acres of land. The tomatoes and cucumbers that Hall buys in the East are probably raised in these gardens," explained Oliver.

"We are now in one of the greatest tomato growing and canning sections of the whole country," he continued. "You should see the trucks come in with loads of tomatoes in the summertime."

"I'd like some tomato juice right now," said Sherman.

"How many are ready to eat?" asked Oliver looking at his watch. "I have made plans to have dinner with some friends, and we are very near their farm."

"Will it be served 'country style'?" asked Mark.

"Wait and see," said Oliver. A half-hour later he told Sherman to stop at the next house on the right.

John Sherman parked the car in front of a big brick farmhouse. There were many maple trees in the yard and a honeysuckle vine in bloom by the door. James Oliver had telephoned the Allen family that he wanted Tom Hall to see what a modern Indiana farm was like. Jenny Allen had invited the whole party for dinner.

The Allen's farm gave the visitors a good picture of farms in Indiana. Their one hundred and sixty acres was not a large farm, but it was a well-managed one. Dave and Jenny Allen did almost all the work with the help of their two boys who went to high school.

Jenny Allen had many machines that made her housework easier than it was in the early pioneer homes. She had an electric washer, ironer, sewing machine, sweeper, stove, and refrigerator.

Dinner was served on the screened porch. There were fresh vegetables, fried chicken, country ham, homemade bread, freshly churned butter, cherry pie, and plenty of milk. The food was put on the table and each one could have as many helpings as he wanted. James Oliver told Mark that this was what "country style" meant—having all the food put on the table at one time and each one taking the amount he wanted. This plan of serving made one feel that people in the country had plenty of good things to eat.

After dinner Dave Allen showed the men some of his new machinery. There was a tractor that could pull almost anything. There were steel plows and a combine, which was a harvesting machine that cut the grain and threshed it at the same time. There were seeders and cultivators. An electric motor furnished the power to grind the grain and pump the water.

"With electricity and all these new machines in the house and in the fields, we have time to read, go to the movies, and take a little vacation trip every year," said Allen. "I want you to see the calf that I plan to take to the state fair. I hope to get a blue ribbon," he added, pointing to a coal-black calf.

After visiting with the Allen family the party said good-by, and again started south on Highway 41.

Using a Road Map

Bring a road map of Indiana to school if you can.

1. Find Highway 40, the old National Road. Through what cities of Indiana does it run?

2. Find Highway 41 which runs north and south through Terre Haute. How many miles is it from Terre Haute to Vincennes?

3. Find Highway 59 which runs north and south through Brazil. What did the party see when they went south on Highway 59 a few miles?

Interesting Things to Do

Make a farm scrapbook. Collect or draw pictures of farm animals, farm machines, and farm crops. Find pictures of plowing, planting, and harvesting.

Visit a farm if you are near one. Go into the barns and sheds. Go into the buildings where the corn, hay, and other crops are stored. Name the fruit trees in the orchard and the vegetables in the garden.

Using New Words

Copy the sentences, filling the blanks with these words:

combine	tractor	vacuum cleaner
refrigerator	cultivator	agriculture

1. A machine that cuts and threshes wheat at the same time is a _____.

2. A machine that keeps food and milk cool is a _____.

3. A machine that sweeps rugs and carpets is a _____.

4. A machine that breaks up the ground and gets rid of weeds is a _____.

5. A machine that takes the place of horses to pull other machines is a _____.

6. Farming is another word for _____.

Finding Answers to Questions

Write the answers to these questions on your paper:

1. What are the main farm crops in Indiana?

2. What are five machines Dave Allen used in farming?

3. What machines did Jenny Allen use to make her housework easier?

4. What power do many farmers have to pump water and run machines?

5. What are some ways Purdue University helps farm people?

Making Charts

Make three charts on your paper:

    1. Farm Life   2. City Life   3. Farm and City

In the farm chart, write the names of farm crops, farm animals, and farm machines that are found on Indiana farms.

FARM LIFE		
Farm Crops	Farm Animals	Farm Machines

In the city chart, write the names of factories, different kinds of stores, and places to go in Indiana cities.

CITY LIFE		
Factories	Stores	Places to Go

On the farm and city chart, write a list of the things city people get from the farm in the first row. In the second row write a list of the things farm people get from the city.

FARM AND CITY	
What city people get from the farm	What farm people get from the city

14. Spring Mill Park

"That visit with the Allens is something to remember," said Hall as he settled back in the car. "Dave Allen knows how to run a farm and Mrs. Allen is a wonderful cook. I never ate better fried chicken, ham, and cherry pie."

"Right you are," chuckled Oliver. "I knew you would like to stop there. The Allens are fine people. They are real Hoosiers."

"I have often wondered where the word, 'Hoosier,' came from," said Hall. "What does it mean?"

"No one knows for sure," replied Oliver. "One story is that the early settlers called 'Who's yere?' when they heard a rap at their door. They wanted to know whether a friend or an enemy was at the door before they opened it. Because of this custom, people in Indiana came to be called, Hoosiers."

"Every citizen of Indiana likes to be called a Hoosier," added Sherman, "for the word has come to mean a person who is friendly and sincere."

"I understand exactly," laughed Hall.

"When you brought me to your home, in place of taking me to a hotel, you were a real Hoosier."

"Thank you," smiled Sherman. "The Allens are real Hoosiers, too. You will meet many others while you are visiting us."

For two hours they drove by peach and apple orchards, acres of melon vines, and fields of tomato plants. When they reached Vincennes, Mark begged them to visit the George Rogers Clark Memorial and the Old Church. He told them some of the things he had learned at school about the early days in Vincennes, as they stood on the bridge over the Wabash River.

After a short rest at Vincennes, the party started east into the hill country. From every hilltop and around each bend in the road was a beautiful view of woods and green valleys.

"There is nothing more beautiful than trees!" exclaimed Hall.

"Or more useful," added Oliver. "The people in Indiana know that now. In the pioneer days great hardwood trees of walnut, maple, and oak were cut down. They were used for houses, for furniture, and to burn in the fireplaces. Much of the wood was wasted.

"There was nothing to hold the soil on the hillsides when the forests were gone. Streams dug deep into the hills and washed away good soil. The farmers saw that if the streams continued to wash it away, they would not have any soil left. They began to plan how to save the forests and the soil. That was the beginning of forest preserves and state parks."

"The state and the United States government became interested and bought thousands of acres of land which could be made into state parks and state and national forest preserves," Sherman added. "Now many of the hardwood trees are saved."

"Were the farmers willing to sell their home places for forest preserves?" asked Hall.

"Most of the farmers gladly sold their land and moved away," said Sherman. "Some of them were allowed to live in their houses for several years after the state bought the land."

"How many forest preserves are there in Indiana?" inquired Hall.

"There are twelve now," replied Sherman, "and each year the state buys more land. The forest preserves cover thousands of acres of land. Many of the preserves are in southern Indiana. Men who have been trained to take care of trees are in charge of them. The men decide which trees are to be cut down and used. They protect the young trees, and they raise millions of seedlings, or baby trees, every year. Because of their work Indiana will never be without trees."

"The men watch for forest fires, too," said Mark. "There are tall watchtowers in all the forests."

"A hundred different kinds of trees and bushes grow in the parks and forest preserves," said Sherman. "Let's see if Mark can tell us some of the more common trees in these forests?"

Mark began to name the trees. "There are hickory, walnut, oak, maple, tulip poplar, sycamore, elm, and beech," he said.

When he finished Oliver added, "There are also many smaller trees and bushes. Among these are redbud, dogwood, red haw, crab apple, pawpaw, sassafras, and willow."

"When we get to Spring Mill Park," said Sherman, "we'll take a walk through one of the forests. Then you can name more of the trees and bushes."

The car traveled along the smooth highway till it came to the entrance to Spring Mill Park. John Sherman turned in at the entrance and followed the road signs inside the park till he came to a beautiful stone hotel in the midst of great trees.

"What a beautiful spot in which to spend the night!" exclaimed Hall.

There was time before the evening meal for a walk through the forest. After dinner the men sat on the porch and talked, but Mark went to bed early.

At the breakfast table next morning Mark asked, "Are we going to see the old mill?"

"Yes, we have time for that," said his father. "Mr. Hall will enjoy the pioneer village that has been rebuilt by the state."

When the meal was ended, the party set out for a walk through the park. They visited the old mill first. With a low rumble the great water wheel ground some corn for them. The men each bought a small bag of corn meal.

The general store, the hat shop, the drug shop, and the inn, each told a story of early days in Indiana. The log houses with their homemade furniture told of home life long ago.

After spending an hour in the village, Hall said, "It is a beautiful spot. I see why it was made into a state park."

At ten o'clock the party returned to the hotel for their baggage. They drove northward through Bedford and the

famous limestone region of the state.

Great blocks of stone were being cut and lifted from open places in the ground, called quarries. A powerful machine very much like the ones used in the strip mines was at work. Its arm swung around as it carried a block of limestone to a flatcar on the railroad track. Then the arm swung back for another block.

Clouds of white dust filled the air. Little pieces of rock lay all around the quarries.

"These scraps make good roads," said Oliver, as they stopped near one of the quarries. "The pieces are ground into dust. It is then made into cement for sidewalks and highways."

"The stone quarries explain your excellent system of paved roads," said Hall. "We have driven many miles this week over smooth concrete highways. It would have taken the early settlers months to have made this trip on dirt roads with their horses and wagons."

"These huge blocks of limestone are used for monuments and large buildings all over the United States," said Sherman. "Indiana limestone is well-known everywhere."

The party journeyed on from Bedford toward Bloomington. "This is the home of Indiana University," said Sherman as they approached Bloomington. "Here young men and women study to become doctors, lawyers, teachers, and writers. They can prepare for almost any work they choose."

"What a beautiful campus! What wonderful buildings!" exclaimed Hall, when they came in sight of the university. "How lucky the people are to have such a school provided by the state.

The party drove on over Highway 37 toward Indianapolis, past another forest preserve. About five o'clock the car rolled up to Sherman's home.

"And how was this trip?" asked Mary Sherman.

"A wonderful trip," answered Tom Hall. "I have seen so many interesting things this week that I am sure my report will become a book. We have seen many kinds of farms as well as coal fields and stone quarries. Indiana seems to have everything."

"That is what we think," smiled his hostess.

"I wish Jean could have seen all I did," said Mark. "Our school books are good, but a trip is the best way to learn things. I'll never forget the big steam shovel in the coal mine. It was almost as long as this block."

"Come in and rest, all of you," Mary Sherman said. "You have two hours before dinner."

Finding Answers

Write the answers to these questions on your paper:

1. What are three stories Mark could have told about early days at Vincennes? The first part of your book will help you.
2. What are three duties of the men who take care of the parks and forest preserves?
3. What are two uses of Bedford limestone?

Learning New Words

Match the words and their meanings. Write the words with their meanings:

1. Hoosier _____　　　　the grounds where college buildings are located.
2. campus _____　　　　the name given to a person who lives in Indiana
3. monument _____　　　a hotel in early days
4. inn _____　　　　　　a forest owned and protected by the state, city, or nation
5. forest preserve _____　a store where many things are sold
6. general store _____　　something to help people remember an event or person

Choosing the Right Heading

Write these headings on your paper:

1. Old National Road　　　　　　2. Highway 40 Today

Read the groups of words. Then write each group of words under the right heading:

dirt and gravel road
paved all the way across Indiana
gas stations in the towns
pretty roadside parks
a log schoolhouse

many cars and trucks
some hogs being driven to market
a stagecoach pulled by horses
two boys on bicycles
fences around farms

Using a Road Map

Look at a road map of Indiana.

1. Find Highway 50 which the travelers took at Vincennes. They went east toward Spring Mill Park.
2. Write the name of the state forest which they saw on Highway 50.
3. Find Mitchell, the town near Spring Mill Park. What direction is Spring Mill Park from Mitchell?
4. Find Highway 37 which runs north and south through Mitchell. This is the road the travelers took when they started home toward Indianapolis.
5. What are two cities they passed through on the way home?
6. What is the number of the state highway that is nearest your home?

15. Indianapolis, the Capital City

Thursday morning after breakfast, Tom Hall and John Sherman read the morning paper and talked in the comfortable living room.

"Tell me something about Indianapolis," said Hall. "I have learned a great deal about the industries and farms in the state. I should like to know more about your city."

"As you know, Indianapolis is the capital city with almost four hundred thousand people living here," began Sherman. "It is the largest city in the United States that is not on a good waterway. Our paved highways and railroads take the place of a waterway."

"I have seen many of your broad streets and beautiful homes, but where are the factories?" asked Hall.

"Indianapolis was well-planned. A man who helped plan Washington, D. C., laid out Indianapolis," said Sherman. "The Monument Circle is the center of the city. From it the streets run north, south, east, and west. The old National Road, or Washington Street, is our main street with stores, hotels, and theaters just like every other large city. The factories and packing houses are along the river and south of the city."

"What factories are located in Indianapolis?" asked Hall.

"It is impossible to name all of them. There are more than 800 different factories, mills, and plants — automobile and airplane factories, meat-packing plants, flour mills, canning factories, and places where hose, drugs, and all kinds of machines are made.

"Nor could I name all the products. Some of them are bicycles, trucks, chains, engines for airplanes, roller skates, and popcorn machines."

"Indianapolis must be a busy place," said Hall. "How are all the products shipped to other places?"

"Indianapolis is a very important railroad center," said Sherman. "There are sixteen railroad lines that pass through the city. The Union Station has enough tracks to take care of forty trains at one time. One hundred twenty truck lines that carry products enter the city. The airplanes carry freight as well as passengers. We have five airports.

"Indianapolis has many meetings during the year. The automobile races in May attract visitors from many states. The basketball games in March bring hundreds of young people to the city. Farmers and their families for miles around attend the state fair in September. There are many other meetings, too."

As Sherman finished speaking the telephone rang. A friend called to remind him of their plans for a trip about the city and a luncheon at 12:00 o'clock. Immediately he called to Mark and Jean, "Are you ready? It is time to go."

"Yes, here we are," answered Jean.

Mark and Jean were going to the City Library and the Children's Museum, as their father took Hall to meet the Mayor and some business men.

In a few minutes the two men and the children were on their way downtown.

"Please drive by the library first," said Mark. "I have a book to return. Then we can walk to the museum."

Ten minutes later Sherman stopped in front of the library. Looking at the entrance, Hall remarked, "I see the name, Riley, everywhere."

"It must seem that way to visitors," laughed Sherman. "We are very proud of James Whitcomb Riley, the Hoosier Poet. Some people call him the children's poet, but we grown-ups like his poems, too."

"I like 'Little Orphant Annie,'" said Jean as she jumped out of the car with Mark. "I like to read about goblins, giants, and elves."

Hall smiled and the children waved good-by.

"We have the Riley Hospital for crippled children which was named for Riley," said Sherman. "Indiana has many other famous writers. Edward Eggleston wrote 'The Hoosier Schoolboy' and 'The Hoosier School Master' years ago. Maurice Thompson wrote 'Alice of Old Vincennes' and 'Stories of Indiana' which contain true stories of early days in Indiana. Some of our famous authors are still living. You may have read their books."

"I have read some of them," replied Hall. "You have excellent artists and musicians, too. I have heard the Indianapolis Symphony Orchestra."

"I am glad to hear you say that, Hall," said his host. "Indiana is more than factories, farms, and places of business. We have made it a good place in which to live."

The men arrived at the City Hall on

time and went at once to the Mayor's office.

"These men are some of the real Hoosiers I told you about," said Sherman after the introductions were over. "They will show you the city and tell you more about Indianapolis."

It was a beautiful day and everybody was very friendly. Tom Hall enjoyed every minute of the morning. The trip to the top of the Soldiers' and Sailors' Monument on the Circle gave him a good view of the city. It was easy to locate the stores and office buildings, the State Capitol, the state and city libraries, and the War Memorial. To the south he saw the factory smokestacks, the Union Station, and the railroad yards. To the west and south he saw

packing houses along White River. Then Hall was taken for a short drive through the business section past the state buildings and the World War Memorial.

"The World War Memorial is very beautiful," said Hall as they drove by.

At twelve o'clock the party arrived at a hotel. The luncheon in a private diningroom was a great success. The business men told Tom Hall many interesting things about their city and state. They gave him many booklets and pictures.

It was an honor to have the Governor present. He invited the group to visit the Capitol after the meeting and see a movie of outdoor Indiana.

"We are interested in keeping Indiana a good place in which to live," said the Governor, as they started on their visit to the capitol building. "It requires many laws to take care of the people. They want good schools, good roads, and parks. We want to protect their homes, their health, and the natural resources that will make it possible for them to earn a living. It takes work to look after the government of the people."

Then the Governor asked a guide to take the visitors through some of the offices. In each office were many men and women working for the state. In the Office of Education they met the State Superintendent of Schools.

"Indiana has good schools and colleges," said the State Superintendent. "A long time ago, Caleb Mills went about the state making speeches and talking on the street corners about free public schools. The people listened and laws were made that provided schools for everybody. Today, we have free public schools for children from first grade through high school, and more than thirty colleges for young people."

"I have seen the four state colleges and many public schools," said Hall. "Your school laws must be good."

"Yes," answered the State Superintendent. "The boys and girls in the southern part of the state use many of the same books as those in the northern part of the state. The children in the country, and in the cities, have comfortable, modern buildings with libraries and gymnasiums. Our teachers are well-trained, too."

"We are very proud of our schools in Indiana," said Sherman.

"You have a right to be," agreed Hall.

From the Superintendent's office the visitors went to the Health Office. There they found doctors, nurses, clerks, and many helpers.

"These people help write the health laws that are passed by the Legislature," said the guide. "The laws protect the health of all the citizens. Some of the laws quarantine persons that have scarlet fever, measles, whooping cough, and other diseases that one person can catch from another person. Some of the laws require cities to have pure drinking water, good sewers, pure foods and drugs, and correct weight for everything sold.

"Many men go about the state inspecting dairies, canning factories, meat and food markets, and water systems. They see that things are clean and well taken care of in the country and in the cities.

"Nurses and doctors in every community teach mothers how to take care of their children and look after those who are sick. The nurses and health workers go into the homes, the schools, and the hospitals to teach people how to keep healthy."

"Health is very important," said Hall. "That is a splendid piece of work."

The visitors moved on to the State Highway Office. The walls were covered with maps. Many people were asking about roads.

"The automobile today makes it necessary for us to keep the roads smooth and in good repair," said the guide. "It is not like it was in the early days of dirt and gravel roads. Every year new paved roads are built."

"Does the state build all of them?" asked Hall.

"The state builds most of them, with some help from the national government," said the guide. "Some of the cities and towns build and repair their streets. It takes engineers, surveyors, and thousands of road workers to build the new roads and keep the old ones in repair. There are a gasoline tax, an automobile fee, and the money from the national government to help pay for the roads. We spend about twenty million dollars a year on roads."

"It is money well-spent," said Hall. "I have enjoyed many good roads since I have been in the state. They connect the cities and towns and farms. One morning we met many trucks loaded with hogs and cattle coming into the city."

"Some mornings as many as five hundred trucks come into Indianapolis with hogs and cattle for the meat-packing houses," said the guide. "Every morning hundreds of people drive to their work in the city. The parking lots and garages are full. Some cars are parked underground while others are taken to the upper floors of brick buildings. We have a good traffic system in order to avoid accidents."

"My company will be interested in your good roads," said Hall. "I shall need these maps that show all the highways."

Next the visitors were taken to the Conservation Office where they enjoyed a movie. The movie explained how the natural resources of Indiana are conserved. One man said, "Our health, wealth, and happiness depend upon how well we take care of our natural resources. We know now that we must not use up all the forests, the soil, the water, the minerals, the plants, and the wild animals."

John Sherman asked a man who worked in the Conservation Office to tell about his work. The man said that the people who know about trees take care of the forest preserves in the state. They plant trees when old ones are cut down. They raise seedlings and take care of saplings. These young trees are sold to farmers in the state. He said that more than three million trees are planted each year.

"Are the state parks a part of your work?" asked Sherman.

"Yes," said the man. "State parks, memorials, fish and game preserves as well as forests are a part of our work. Beautiful scenic places in Indiana have been made into state parks to preserve the trees, flowers, birds, fish and small animals. Large fish hatcheries supply many different kinds of fish for small lakes and streams. A farmer can get bass or perch for a lake on his farm. Laws to control fishing and hunting have been made.

"Some men get rid of mosquitoes, flies, and insects that destroy trees and crops," continued the conservation man. "Other men get rid of weeds and harmful plants like poison ivy.

"Our magazine, 'Outdoor Indiana,' is sent free to anyone interested in conserving the plants, animals, soil, and minerals of Indiana. Here are some copies for you," he added, handing a magazine to each visitor. "They will tell you about the conservation program in the state."

At four o'clock the party completed the trip through the offices in the State Capitol. Sherman and Hall piled the booklets they had collected into the Sherman car and started home.

Finding Answers

Copy these sentences, filling the blanks with words from the story:

Indianapolis is the _____ of our state. More than _____ people live in Indianapolis. Some of the products made in the factories are _____, _____, and _____. There are _____ railroad lines, _____ truck lines, and _____ airports.

Many meetings are held in Indianapolis. In May there are _____. In the winter there are _____. In the fall there is a _____.

The Governor of our state is _____. His office is in the _____. The laws that protect the people are passed by the _____. The people in the State Highway Office see that the _____ are repaired and new ones built. The people in the Conservation Office employ people to take care of _____, _____, and _____.

Remembering the Laws of Indiana

Indiana has many state laws that people should know and obey. You have learned many of them at home and at school. How well do you remember some of the laws?

1. There are health laws which the school nurse and doctor help you to keep. Name three health laws on your paper.
2. There are traffic laws you keep when crossing the street. The safe driver keeps many traffic laws. Name three traffic laws of Indiana on your paper.
3. There are laws about attending school. Name three school laws.

Learning New Words

Read the meanings of these new words. Then see if you can use them correctly in sentences:

1. Natural resources: The soil, the water supply, the forests and all the animals, plants, and minerals make up the natural resources of a region. The people of Indiana use the natural resources to get food, clothing, and shelter. Some of the natural resources of Indiana are _____, _____, and _____.

2. Monument: A piece of stone, a building, or a statue that helps people remember a person, a great piece of work, or an important place may be called a monument. The Soldiers' and Sailors' Monument on the circle in Indianapolis is to remind the people of the soldiers and sailors who fought for our country. The World War Memorial is a _____.

3. Museum: A building where a collection of objects is kept is called a museum. Usually the objects are named so people can look at them and read about them. The Children's Museum in Indianapolis has a collection of furniture, clothes, and tools which were used by the pioneers long ago. The museums at the state parks have collections of rocks that are found in the parks. A school museum often has _____.

4. Conserve: To keep things from being wasted means to conserve them. The people of Indiana use coal, trees, and all the natural resources with care. At school, children can conserve _____.

Famous People of Indiana

Indiana has many famous writers. Some have written stories and poems for children and some have written books for grown-ups. Make a list of these writers. Give the title of a story or a book that each one wrote. Put a star before the name of each writer who wrote books for children.

*Miriam Mason	Smiling Hill Farm
Booth Tarkington	Gentleman from Indiana
Edward Eggleston	Hoosier School-boy

James Whitcomb Riley was the Hoosier Poet. If you can, bring a book of his poems to class. If you do not have a book, copy a poem to read to the class. Write the titles of five of Riley's poems.

Using a Map of Indianapolis

Look at the map of the business part of Indianapolis.

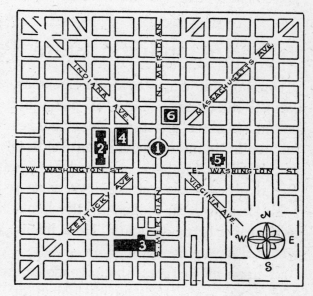

1. Locate the circle, which is the center of the city.

2. Find the Capitol Building, west of the circle.

3. Find the Union Station, south of the circle.

4. Find the Terminal Bus Station, west of the circle.

5. Find the Marion County Courthouse, east of the circle.

6. Find the Post Office, north of the circle.

7. Find Washington Street. It is the same as Highway 40, but it is called Washington Street within the city limits of Indianapolis.

8. A block from the circle, find the four main avenues that run northeast, southeast, northwest, and southwest.

9. Copy these sentences, filling the blanks with the right direction words:

    Massachusetts Avenue runs _____.

    Virginia Avenue runs _____.

    Kentucky Avenue runs _____.

    Indiana Avenue runs _____.

16. Indiana State Parks and Memorials

On the following day John Sherman went to his office to look after some important business matters. Tom Hall remained at home to sort the pictures and booklets that had been given to him. He was ready to start writing his report.

Mark and Jean looked at the booklets and pictures while Hall busily wrote a few pages.

"I need more facts about roads and highways," said Hall as he looked at what he had written.

"Here are some booklets and maps on highways," said Mark. "We use road maps when we drive to the lake every summer."

"We go to the state parks for picnics, too," said Jean. "It is fun to wade in the streams and walk along the trails through the woods. On hot summer days the parks are full of people."

"How many state parks are there in Indiana?" asked Hall.

"There are fourteen state parks and many memorials," replied Mark. "We could play a geography game, if you have time. I'll name a park and the town or city near it. Jean can tell in which part of the state it is. You can find it on the map, Mr. Hall."

"That's fine," said Tom Hall, as he took the highway map of Indiana.

"Turkey Run," called Mark. "It is near Rockville and Marshall. Once there were hundreds of flocks of wild turkeys there. That is why it is called Turkey Run."

"It is in the central part of Indiana," said Jean, "But it is on the west side, too."

"I have it," said Hall.

"Clifty Falls," called Mark. "It is near Madison."

"That is in the southern part," said Jean, "on the Ohio River where you can see the steamboats."

"Here it is. I think I shall see it when we take our trip through southern Indiana."

"McCormick's Creek State Park," said Mark. "It was the first state park. There are beech, oak, maple, and pine trees there. A guide will tell you all about the rocks, birds, and trees."

"It is in the center," said Jean. "Once we swam in a pool at that park."

"But what town is it near?" asked Hall.

"It is near Spencer and Bloomington," said Jean.

They played the game until all the parks were named and located. Spring Mill State Park is near Mitchell in the southern part of the state. It has the pioneer village and old mill with a big water wheel. Dunes State Park is in the northern part of the state on Lake Michigan. It is close to Gary. People go there who like to swim and picnic on the white, sandy beach. Shakamak (Shak'-a-mak) State Park is in the southwestern part of the state near Jasonville. Shakamak Lake is a very good place to swim and fish. Brown County State Park, the one the artists like, is near Nashville in the south central part of the state.

Mounds State Park is near Anderson in the central part of the state. In that park are many paths up and down the hills through the woods. Pokagon (Po-kay'-gon) State Park has two large lakes, Lake James and Snow Lake. It is near Angola in the northeastern corner of the state. It was named for an Indian chief. Bass Lake State Park is a small park in the northern part of the state. Families enjoy camping and fish-ing there. Lincoln State Park in the southern part of the state is where Abraham Lincoln lived for fourteen years. Muscatatuck (Mus-cat'-a-tuck) State Park has an old quarry and an old dam. It is near North Vernon.

Tippecanoe River State Park contains more than six thousand acres of land along the Tippecanoe River near Winnemac, in the north central part of the state. It has many trails, picnic places, and camping grounds. Versailles State Park is in southern Indiana near Versailles. It, too, has thousands of acres of land for picnic and camping grounds.

"Where are the memorials?" asked Hall as they finished locating the parks.

"We can play a history game with them," said Mark. "Each memorial stands for something important in the history of Indiana."

"That will be hard," frowned Jean. "It will take too long."

"Don't tell the whole story," laughed Mark. "Just tell why it was chosen for a memorial."

"I'll call the memorial," said Jean. "And you tell the story."

"Turn about, fair play," said Hall. "I'll locate it and Mark can tell the story."

"Nancy Hanks Lincoln Memorial," called Jean.

"It is in Lincoln State Park," said Mark. "It is to remind people of Abraham Lincoln's mother. Her grave is there, and a cabin like the one in which the Lincolns lived."

"The Lanier Home," said Jean.

"It was the home of James Lanier, in Madison. He was a very wealthy man who lent money to the state when it was needed. The garden and yard reach to the Ohio River. The furniture in the house is arranged as if the family still lived there."

"Corydon State Capital and the Constitution Elm," said Jean.

"Corydon was the first capital of Indiana," said Mark. "The old capitol building where the first laws were made is still there. A stone marks the place where the Constitution Elm stood."

"Pigeon Roost Memorial," said Jean.

"It tells the story of an Indian raid on the white settlers," said Mark. "The white men and Indians had been friendly for several months. Then one day two hunters were killed by some Indians. That night the Indians killed another man, five women, and sixteen children. The memorial is in the southern part of the state."

"The New Harmony Memorial, Old Goshen Church, Deam Oak, the T. C. Steele Memorial, the Wilbur Wright Birthplace, the George Rogers Clark Memorial, and the Tippecanoe Battlefield Memorial are the others," said Jean, as they folded their maps.

"The New Harmony Memorial is for a group of people who tried out some new ways of living together in the southern part of Indiana," Mark continued. "It is in New Harmony. Dad says it will soon be a state memorial. The Tippecanoe Battlefield Memorial is on the battlefield where Governor William Henry Harrison defeated the Indian tribes. It is at Battle Ground near Lafayette.

"Old Goshen Church is one of the pioneer churches. Many famous pioneers and Revolutionary War soldiers lie buried in the old church cemetery. Deam Oak is a fine oak tree which the state wishes to preserve. It is on a small piece of land near Bluffton. The T. C. Steele Memorial contains many beautiful paintings by T. C. Steele, the Brown County artist, who gave his farm and studio to the state. It is near Bloomington.

"The Wilbur Wright Birthplace is in Henry County near New Castle," Mark added. "Wilbur Wright helped invent and fly one of the first airplanes. The George Rogers Clark Memorial at Vincennes is to remind us of the many brave deeds of Clark in the early days of Indiana."

"We have seen nearly all the state parks," said Jean. "Dad says he will take us to see some of the memorials this summer on our vacation trip."

"Indiana would be a good vacation place," said Hall. "I think my family would enjoy your parks and memorials, too. You have been a great help. Now I must put down some of these things in my report."

Tom Hall gathered up the booklets and carried them to his room. Then he wrote several pages. He knew his company wanted to build some new fac-

tories so he jotted down these reasons why Indiana is a good place for factories: (1) many materials that could be made into products; (2) water, coal, and electric power to run the factories; (3) many railroads, waterways, highways; (4) many workers; and (5) many people to buy products.

At the end of this report he put down a number of statements about Indiana. He took these from a Chamber of Commerce booklet and booklets from Indiana's Department of Commerce and Public Relations.

Using a Map

Find the state parks and memorials on the map of Indiana.

STATE PARKS

1. McCormick's Creek
2. Turkey Run
3. Muscatatuck
4. Clifty Falls
5. Indiana Dunes
6. Pokagon
7. Brown County
8. Shakamak
9. Spring Mill
10. The Mounds
11. Bass Lake Beach
12. Lincoln
13. Tippecanoe River
14. Versailles

MEMORIALS

15. Tippecanoe Battlefield
16. James F. D. Lanier
17. Corydon State Capitol
18. Nancy Hanks Lincoln
19. Pigeon Roost
20. Deam Oak
21. The T. C. Steele
22. Old Goshen Church
23. George Rogers Clark
24. Wilbur Wright Birthplace
25. Constitution Elm
26. New Harmony

Fun in the Parks

Write the name of each park on your paper and tell one thing you can see or one thing you can do at the park.

Trees in Indiana

Write a list of trees under the right heading:

    1. Fruit Trees   2. Trees for Lumber and for Shade

Finding the Answer

Write four things about which a company asks when it wants to find a good place to build a new factory.

Facts About Indiana

Location: Middle West—near the center of the nation. Crossed by many important east-west and north-south railroads. Leading national highways cross the state.

Capital: The capital, near the center of the state, is Indianapolis. About 400,-000 people. 800 different factories.

Population: In 1943—3,383,312 people in Indiana.

Industries: 4,350 industries employ about 318,400 workers.

Products: Steel and iron products, automobile bodies and parts, railroad-materials, foundry and machine-shop products, radios and radio parts, food and meat products, clothing, hosiery, drugs.

Value of products is about $2,227,650,000.

Value of property in the state is about $3,852,140,000.

Agriculture: Some 184,500 farms contain about 19,800,780 acres. Deep, rich, clay loam soil. Rainfall and temperature make good growing seasons.

Natural Resources: Twelve state forests, four game preserves, eight fish hatcheries.

Many native forests, rich coal fields, sand and gravel beds, clay for tile and brick, and limestone quarries.

Government: Changes to meet the needs of the people and times. Good system of education, roads and highways, public health, conservation of natural resources, state parks, and state memorials.

17. A Trip Through Southern Indiana

Clifty Falls

"We're going to Clifty Falls! We're going to Clifty Falls!" sang Jean, as Mark came in from play later in the afternoon.

"That's great," said Mark. "We'll see the boats on the Ohio River. Are we going with Dad and Mr. Hall?"

"Yes, and Mother is going, too," answered Jean. "Mother is packing the suitcases now."

"I'll take my bird book," said Jean.

"I'll get my road map," said Mark.

"Put them with your coats in the hall," said their mother as she finished packing. "Let's take care of the flowers now. They must have plenty of water, if we are to be gone a few days."

John Sherman found them in the garden when he came home from the office. A few minutes later their guest came out of the house.

"Did you get your report written?" asked Sherman.

"I have almost finished it," Hall re-plied. "And how was your day at the office?"

"A very busy one," said Sherman, "but I have everything in good shape again."

"Do you take care of the flowers?" asked Hall, turning to Mary Sherman. "You have many flowers—roses, pansies, daisies, and lilies."

"We all like flowers so everyone helps take care of them," his hostess replied.

"It is nice to have a flower garden," said Hall. "In the large cities in the East we don't have yards and gardens as you have here in the Middle West."

"I know," said Mary Sherman. "That is one more reason why we like Indiana. There is plenty of land here for yards and gardens."

Mark and Jean watered the flowers while the others went into the house. A little later when the supper things were put away, the children went into the livingroom with their mother.

Jean yawned as she picked up a book. Just then her mother said, "It is time for bed now. You must get a good night's sleep so you will enjoy the drive tomorrow."

Mark and Jean skipped off to bed, for they knew they would be up early the next morning.

Sure enough, they were up bright and early, ready to go. They carried their suitcases to the livingroom. After breakfast their father brought the car from the garage. By half past nine everyone was ready to start.

Tom Hall sat in front with John Sherman. Jean and Mark climbed into the back seat with their mother. The sun shone brightly as the party headed south through the city and out into the country on Highway 31.

They enjoyed looking at the green fields, the barnyards full of chickens and pigs, and the trees on the hillsides. They had lunch at a hotel in a small town, and then drove on. It was three o'clock in the afternoon when the car stopped at the entrance to Clifty Falls State Park. After getting the tickets and a map of the park, they drove up the steep hill to the hotel.

Mark and Jean could hardly wait to see the Ohio River from the front porch of the hotel. A big, paddle-wheeled steamboat was near the bend of the river. Another boat was coming into view up the river. It was fun to watch the boats steam down the river and go out of sight around the bend.

"Shall we take a walk?" asked their father, as he came out on the porch a few minutes later.

"Oh, yes!" cried Mark. "Let's take the trail to the falls."

The party followed the trail to the falls. Many young birds flew about. Now and then a chipmunk ran across the path. The grown-ups rested on the park benches when they reached the falls. But Mark and Jean continued to run up and down the hills and play under the trees.

"Come, rest awhile before we return," called their mother an hour later. "It is almost suppertime."

"Let's make bird riddles," cried Jean picking up her bird book from the park bench.

"That is a fine game," said her mother. "Give us one to guess."

Jean said, "I am thinking of a bird that is almost all red. It has a little black on its face. There is a topknot on its head. What is it?"

"That is too easy," Mark told her. "It is the redbird, or cardinal. Everybody knows that one for it is our state bird. Here is a hard one. I'm thinking of a bird that belongs to the woodpecker family. It does not have a red head. The underside of its wings and its tail are bright yellow. It hammers on trees. It digs out its nest in a pole or tree. What is it?"

"I give up," said Jean after a few minutes. "A red-headed woodpecker is the only one in that family that I know."

"A yellow hammer!" cried Mark.

"Here is a different kind of riddle," said their mother. "Name two birds that belong to the blackbird family. Now, remember a bird does not have to be all black to belong to the blackbird family."

"Red-winged blackbird," said Jean.

"Meadowlark," said Mark.

"Good," said their mother. "The oriole belongs to the blackbird family, too. I see you both learned about the common birds of Indiana in your class at school."

"Oh, yes," said Mark. "We collected bird's nests, and we made a list of all the birds of Indiana."

"Let's see how many you can name," said his mother.

After Mark and Jean had named as many birds as they could, their mother told them how birds are protected in the parks and woods.

On the way back to the hotel, their father stopped suddenly and motioned for the children to stand still. He pointed to a family of quails under a beech tree. The mother quail made a low sound and all the little ones sat as still as stones. It was hard to see them among the leaves and grass.

Soon after supper the children went to bed, but the grown-ups talked awhile longer.

Next morning the party started on its way at eight o'clock. The road took them in sight of the Ohio River many times. It took them through forests and farm lands.

"Our first stop is New Albany," said Sherman. "It is one of the oldest towns in the state. Many of the first settlers floated down the Ohio on flatboats and settled there. The town stretches about two miles along the north bank of the Ohio River. It depends upon the river for trade and shipping as well as upon the railroads."

"Is there much shipping now?" asked Hall as they reached Market Street and drove slowly through the city.

"Yes," said Sherman. "There are steamboat lines from Pittsburg to New Orleans. New Albany is still a lumber market. There are sawmills and plywood mills. There are other factories, too. Some of the products are boilers, stokers, and stoves. Very fine suits, overcoats, and shirts are made here, too."

"Do they build boats now?" asked

Mark. "We learned at school that in the early days many boats were made in New Albany."

"Not as many are made today," said his father. "In the early days shipbuilding was the main business. The famous *Robert E. Lee* that won the boat race on the Mississippi River was built in New Albany. The boats raced between St. Louis and New Orleans on their way to the big market. In those days many steamboat captains and their families came to live in New Albany. Every captain wanted to see that his boat was well built."

"I suppose the railroads have taken some of the shipping business," said Hall.

"Yes." said Sherman, "not so many boats were needed, so the lumber companies began to use the lumber for furniture and houses."

After a short stop at one of the lumber companies, Sherman drove on. Very soon he came to Corydon, the first capital of Indiana.

"The old State Capitol is here," said Jean. "This is where the first laws in Indiana were made. It was in the summertime and the men met outdoors under an elm tree."

"The capital was soon moved to Indianapolis," said Sherman. "The people in the northern part of the state thought Corydon was too far south."

The car passed through Corydon, and sped along through the wooded hills and valleys for many miles.

"This is one of the forest preserves of the United States," said Sherman as they drove past a great forest. "The government of the United States has some forest preserves in Indiana, too."

At noon the party stopped at Lincoln State Park to eat a picnic lunch which the Clifty Falls Hotel had packed for them. Later they visited the grave of Lincoln's mother at the Nancy Hanks Lincoln Memorial.

"Indiana is proud to claim Lincoln as one of its great men," said Sherman, "although he spent only a part of his boyhood in the state."

As the party drove on toward Evansville they left the hills. The land became level. Fields of grain and pasturelands were seen. Late in the afternoon the car brought them along the river road into Evansville.

"Evansville is quite a trade center," said Sherman. "Many big companies have factories in Evansville. Steam shovels, electric and gas refrigerators, furniture, and automobiles are only a few of the products made here."

"How large is Evansville?" inquired Hall.

"About a hundred thousand people

live in Evansville," answered Sherman. "There are more than two hundred factories that hire thousands of workers."

"People who like cakes should know that a very good cake flour is made here," laughed Mary Sherman.

"Soft wheat for flour is one of the best crops in this part of the state," said Sherman. "That is why the mills make cake flour."

"The city is famous for its baby food, too," said Mary Sherman. "It is sold all over this country and in many other parts of the world. It is easily shipped down the Ohio and the Mississippi to New Orleans. From there it is taken to South America and Cuba."

"A man from Sweden has the patent for one of the refrigerators made here," said Sherman. "Evansville has much business with places far away."

"This is very interesting," said Hall, making notes.

Then John Sherman told about the waterway-highway-railway terminal trade building. He said that products are brought to the terminal by trains, trucks, boats, and barges. From there the goods are shipped to other parts of the country and to other nations.

"I must see the terminal trade building tomorrow," said Hall as the car stopped at the hotel where the party spent the night.

Evansville on the Ohio River

"Come, Mark, look out the window," called Jean next morning. "Hurry!"

Mark ran to the window from which there was a splendid view of the Ohio River. He was in time to see a big boat pulling a long string of low, flat-bottomed boats called barges.

"Get dressed, quickly!" cried Mark. "I don't want to miss the trip to the terminal building. That is where the boats are going."

Mark, Jean, and their mother joined the men for breakfast. "What are your plans for the day?" Mary Sherman asked when she was seated.

"We are going to the terminal trade building first," her husband replied. "You, Mark, and Jean will enjoy that. Then Hall and I shall visit some of the factories and get a view of the city."

"Oh, goody!" said Jean. "We saw a string of boats on the river this morning."

"Mark can go with us this morning," said his father.

"Gee, that's the time!" cried Mark.

"We'll all meet at the hotel for lunch at one o'clock," continued Sherman. "Soon after that we shall start home."

As soon as breakfast was over the party drove to the terminal trade building. Men were loading some barges with machines and large boxes. A big steamboat was waiting to pull them down the river. A train of cars was being unloaded on the other side of the building. Some of the goods were taken from the train to the boats. The clerk at the terminal trade building explained that it was cheaper to send some things by boat than on trains and trucks. He said that many factories in the northern part of the state ship their products to Evansville by train. At Evansville the products are sent on boats to New Orleans. Then the clerk showed them the trucks. Some of the trucks had products to be shipped south on the boats. Other trucks had products to be sent north on the trains. The trade terminal was a very busy place.

After watching the work for an hour, Jean and her mother went shopping. The two men and Mark drove to an airplane factory.

Sherman explained that during World War II, Evansville produced many products for the war. A large airplane factory made fighter planes used in Europe and the Pacific Islands.

Another factory made heavy boats that landed men and tanks in Europe and the Pacific Islands. Huge steam shovels like those used in strip mines were sent to China and Africa. They were used to make roads and to make landing fields for airplanes.

The car paused at the entrance to the airplane factory and the gateman motioned for them to park near the office building.

"We have a pleasant surprise for you," said the manager of the factory when they entered his office. "We can take you for a short airplane trip over the city and countryside."

"That is a surprise!" said Sherman. "Now, we can see the whole city in a short time. Is there room for three passengers?"

"Oh, yes," said the manager as he stepped to the door and motioned to the pilot that they were ready.

It was Mark's first trip in an airplane, but he did not say a word. He thought he might be afraid when the plane left the ground, but he wasn't. The plane left the ground smoothly. They all looked out of the windows. Far below were the houses, streets, and factories. The plane circled the city and went out over the river.

"Why is the river so muddy?" asked Mark.

"The rain has washed good soil from the farms into the streams," said his father. "The streams have carried it to the river. And the river is carrying it on to the ocean. That is why the farmers plant trees to hold their soil."

"This is a splendid way to see the city!" said Hall.

"It certainly is," said Sherman. "You can see why Evansville is a great trade center. It is in the heart of farm lands and coal fields."

The trip lasted only half an hour. The pilot made a wide circle and gave them a good view of the city and its industries.

"Won't Jean and Mother be surprised when I tell them about my plane ride?" asked Mark as they climbed out of the plane.

"Yes, they will," said his father. "After we have talked with the manager of the factory we shall drive past a few of these places and see how they look from the ground."

Mark talked with the pilot and admired the plane while the men visited the factory and talked with the manager.

On the way back to the hotel they saw the gas and electric refrigerator factories, a cigar plant, and some of the furniture factories.

"I can see why big companies in the East and North have factories in Evansville," said Hall. "I am glad we made this trip. Every part of Indiana has something different to offer."

"Perhaps your company will want to build many factories in Indiana," said Sherman.

"I am sure it will," replied Hall.

Mark could hardly wait to tell about the airplane ride over the city. His mother and Jean enjoyed his story very much.

After lunch the bags were put in the back of the car and the party started home on Highway 57. At sundown they were back home in Indianapolis.

Writing Letters

Write to the Evansville Chamber of Commerce for booklets about the city and its industries.

Write sentences about Evansville by filling the blanks with words from the story.

Evansville is in the southern part of Indiana on the _____. More than _____ people live there. The big factories make _____, _____, _____, and _____. Some of the baby food is shipped to _____. On the Ohio River is a terminal trade building where goods are shipped by _____, _____, and _____.

Common Birds of Indiana

You already know a great many birds that live near your home. Many of them are common to all parts of Indiana. Make a bird chart or booklet of birds. Make a list of Indiana birds.

Drawing Pictures

Draw three pictures to show travel on the Ohio River long ago and today. The sentences below give you hints for your pictures.

1. The early settlers floated down the Ohio on flatboats with all their household goods to settle in southern Indiana.
2. The steamboats carried the products of the farms to market.
3. Steamboats with strings of barges carry products to New Orleans.

Finding the Answers

Copy the sentences from the story that answer these questions:

1. Why do factories ship some of their products by boats to New Orleans?
2. What did one of the airplane factories make?
3. Where were the huge steam shovels sent?
4. What was the pleasant surprise for the visitors?
5. Why was the Ohio River muddy?
6. What did Mark do while his father talked with the manager of the airplane factory?

18. The Visitor Returns Home

"I'll never forget my trip to Indiana," said Tom Hall, as he came down to breakfast the last morning. "I have learned a great deal about the state. I know why the people are called Hoosiers, and I can see why Indiana is called the 'Crossroads of America.'"

"I'm glad you like our state," said Mary Sherman. "We have all enjoyed your visit. Perhaps you will be coming again."

"I hope so," replied the guest. "My report is sure to bring some factories to the state. Indiana has much to offer and it is a good place in which to live. Trains, airplanes, and cars make us neighbors. Here I am having breakfast with you in the Middle West. This evening I shall have dinner at my home in the East, which is several hundred miles away. The airplane is a great invention."

"We have a gift for you," said Mark as they left the table. "Jean and I have made a small scrapbook of Indiana for your son. We hope he likes it."

"I am sure he will," said Hall as he thanked the children and opened the book. "Where did you get all the pictures?"

"The State Historical Bureau gave them to us," said Jean. "The pictures and stories about Indiana are given to school children so they will know more about their state. In the State Library are hundreds of books about Indiana, too."

While Sherman brought the car, Hall turned the pages of the book, and read What Mark and Jean had written:

Indiana State Motto: The Crossroads of America.

The State Song

The State Song is *On The Banks Of The Wabash, Far Away*. It was written by Paul Dresser, who spent his boyhood in Indiana.

The State Banner

The **Daughters** of the American Revolution offered a prize for the best design for a state banner. A blue banner with a gold torch and nineteen gold stars was chosen. The torch stands for liberty. The outer circle of thirteen stars stands for the thirteen colonies that became the first thirteen states of the United States. The inner circle of five stars stands for the next five states to come into the United States. The large star just above the torch stands for Indiana which was the nineteenth state.

The State Bird

The redbird, or cardinal, is the state bird. It whistles and sings in the low trees and bushes the year around. The mother cardinal is brown with touches of red on her wings and head. The male bird is red with a topknot on his head.

The State Tree

The tulip tree is the state tree. It is one of the largest trees in Indiana. In May or June it has large greenish yellow flowers that look like tulips. It grows best when planted in the spring. Its soft white wood has many uses.

The State Flower

The zinnia is the state flower. It grows in all parts of the state. The most common colors are red, yellow, and orange. Some of the blossoms are large and some are small.

"That is a pretty little book," said Tom Hall as he tucked it away in his suitcase. "I know my son will enjoy it."

Just then John Sherman drove up, ready to take him to the airport. The good-bys were said and the car rolled out of the driveway. In a short time the men reached the airport.

"I want to thank you for all you have done this week," Hall said, as he told Sherman good-by. "It was a great pleasure to be in your home and to know your family. My company will appreciate what you and the Chambers of Commerce have done. With your help I have been able to collect all the important facts needed. I feel sure more than one of our factories will be located in your state."

"The Chamber of Commerce will be pleased," Sherman replied. "We enjoyed having you with us. It has been like a little vacation trip to me. Why don't you bring your family and spend a week at one of the state parks?"

"I've been thinking about it," replied Hall. "Indiana is a real vacation place. As Mrs. Sherman said, 'Indiana has everything.' Indiana really is the 'Crossroads of America.'"

Making An Outline

Write two or three interesting facts under each topic heading. Then you will have an outline to help you remember about living in Indiana today.

1. Rivers in Indiana
2. Weather and Climate in Indiana
3. Farm Crops in Indiana
4. Large Cities in Indiana
5. Products of Factories in Indiana
6. Ways of Traveling in Indiana

Pictures for Your Book

Write to the State Historical Bureau, in Indianapolis, for pictures of the State Banner, the State Tree, the State Flower, the State Bird, and the State Motto.

Make a picture to go with the State Song.

Writing Letters

Write the note you think Jean and Mark put in the scrapbook they sent to Tom Hall's son.

Write the thank-you note you think Mr. Hall's son wrote to Jean and Mark for the scrapbook.

DIRECTIONS FOR USING THE BOOK

To the Teacher

LIVING IN INDIANA presents in story form the more general events and movements in the geographical and historical development of Indiana. Every part of Indiana, every city, every little village, and every community has a story of its own. Space does not permit all these stories of Indiana to be told in one book.

Since only the minimum amount of material is presented in this book, it will be necessary and desirable to secure additional information from libraries, trips, movies, pamphlets, posters, and pictures. Supplementary readers and other textbooks provide many stories and factual accounts of life in Indiana.

The bibliography contains books for the children's reading table and background reading for the teacher.

The list of places to write for materials and the suggested approaches indicate equipment and materials necessary for good work.

Planning ahead for activities will deepen the understandings and supplement this book. Those activities which appeal to the interests of individuals and the needs of the group should be selected early and carried out as the work progresses.

The study exercises at the end of each chapter provide for the development and maintenance of specific social studies skills. Best results will be obtained if the exercises are supervised by the teacher as a part of the recitation period.

The purposes of this book on Indiana for the elementary schools are, (1) to develop an understanding of living in Indiana today, (2) to build basic history and geography concepts, (3) to increase and broaden the skills of the language arts, (4) to develop certain specific social studies skills, such as, reading maps, acquiring a vocabulary peculiar to the content, and locating supplementary library materials, and (5) to establish a pride and love for our home state, INDIANA.

Selected Books for Children and Teachers

BOOKS RECOMMENDED FOR THE CLASSROOM LIBRARY FOR CHILDREN.

Horn, Madeline, *Log Cabin Family*, 1939, Charles Scribner's Sons, New York 17.

Hunt, Mabel Leigh, *Cornbelt Billy*, 1942, Grosset and Company, New York, 10.

Major, Charles, *Bears of Blue River*, 1925, The Macmillan Company, Chicago, 16.

Mason, Miriam, *Little Jonathan*, 1944, The Macmillan Company, Chicago, 16.

Mason, Miriam, *Smiling Hill Farm*, 1937, Ginn and Company, Chicago, 16.

Mason, Miriam, *Suzannah, The Pioneer Cow*, 1941, The Macmillan Company, Chicago, 16.

Waddell, J. E. and Perry, Amy, *Long Ago*, 1933, The Macmillan Company, Chicago, 16.

Wilder, Laura, *Farmer Boy*, 1933, Harper and Brothers, New York, 16.

BOOKS TO BE READ TO THE CHILDREN.

Eggleston, Edward, *Hoosier School-boy*, 1936, Charles Scribner's Sons, New York.

Hunt, Mabel Leigh, *Lucinda, A Little Girl of 1860*, 1934, J. B. Lippincott Co., Philadelphia, 5.

Lockridge, Ross, *LaSalle*, 1931, World Book Company, Yonkers-on-Hudson, N. Y.

Lockridge, Ross, *George Rogers Clark*, 1927, World Book Company, Yonkers-on-Hudson, N. Y.

Nolan, Jeanette, *Hobnailed Boots*, 1939, John C. Winston Company, Philadelphia, 7.

Sperry, Portia H. and Donaldson, Lois, *Abigail*, 1938, Whitman Company, Chicago, 6.

Thompson, Maurice, *Stories of Indiana*, 1898, American Book Company, New York, 16.

BOOKS FOR THE TEACHER. GENERAL INFORMATION.

Bowman, Heath, *Hoosier*, 1941, The Bobbs-Merrill Company, Indianapolis, 7, Indiana.

Esarey Logan, *A History of Indiana*, Volume I, 1915; Volume II, 1918, Hoosier Press, Fort Wayne, Indiana.

Wilson, William, *The Wabash*, 1940, Rinehart & Co., Inc., New York, 16.

Writers Project, *Indiana, A Guide to the Hoosier State*, 1941, Oxford University Press, New York, 11.

Places to Write for Materials

1. Indiana State Historical Bureau, 406 State Library Building, Indianapolis, Indiana:

   Pamphlets, yearbooks, folders, and pictures of memorials in Indiana. Colored prints of the state seal, bird, tree, flower, and banner.

2. Chambers of Commerce—State and Local:

   Pamphlets, bulletins, maps, and charts containing interesting facts about agriculture and industry, large cities, population, wealth, and means of transportation. Many cities have accounts of the historical development of the city and immediate community.

3. Local Farm Bureau:

   Pamphlets, posters, and bulletins about soil, crops, vegetables, fruits, poultry, stock, and everything concerning farm life.

4. Local, State, and National American Automobile Associations:

   City, state, sectional, and national maps; bulletins, posters, and travel books containing descriptions of highways, hotels, tourist places, parks, memorials, and all places of interest in the state.

5. Local Oil and Gas Companies:

   Road maps and city maps.

6. Outdoor Indiana, Department of Conservation, 406 State Library Building, Indianapolis, Indiana:

   A magazine, published monthly, which contains stories, articles, and many pictures of plant and animal life of Indiana. Conservation of natural resources is stressed. Pamphlets on the state parks and memorials. Motion pictures.

7. Indiana, Department of Commerce and Public Relations, 333 State House, Indianapolis, Indiana:

   Booklets, pamphlets, and maps giving valuable information.

Directed Activities

To THE TEACHER: Directed Activities are addressed to the child, but the teacher should give aid and direction.

I. Plan ahead for some trips. One of the best ways to learn about your state is to see for yourself the places and things about which you read and talk.

1. Visit a park in your community and also the state park nearest you. Name the trees and flowers. Study the land forms and the water supply. Have a good time on the trip and share what you learn with those who were unable to go with you.

2. Visit a memorial in your community. Read about it before you go and tell your friends about it afterward.

3. Take a trip to a city. If the trip is made to Indianapolis, visit the circle and the monument. Visit the Children's Museum. Notice the streets, the schools, the churches, the parks, the homes, and the factories. If there is time, visit a large department store.

    Ask the principal and superintendent to permit the use of the school bus for one trip to be taken on Saturday. Invite some parents to take the trip with you.

    An all-day trip to the country is as valuable for children who live in the city as a trip to a large city is for those in rural communities.

4. Visit at least two factories or places of business in your community to learn more about how people earn a living in Indiana.

5. Take a trip to a typical farm in Indiana. Notice the crops, the stock, and the many farm buildings.

6. Visit some person who likes antiques. You will probably see some old furniture, pictures, household articles, and clothes. Ask about spinning wheels, candle molds, old cradles, and other antiques.

II. Begin a scrapbook on Indiana. Pictures, stories, poems, and clippings from newspapers and magazines will help you remember interesting events.

1. Draw pictures that tell how Indiana changed as the times changed. Paste them in your scrapbook.

2. Find pictures in magazines that show how people live today. Paste them opposite the ones that show how people lived long ago.

3. Copy some poems about Indiana. Paste them in your book. Draw some pictures for them. Try to write some poems yourself.

4. Write a story about something you like in Indiana and draw some pictures for your story.

5. Keep a list of poems, stories, and books about Indiana that you have read.

6. Read the newspaper to find interesting stories of Indiana people and happenings. Clip them from the paper and paste them in your book.

7. Read some stories from *Outdoor Indiana*. Re-write the stories for your scrapbook.

III. Begin to paint a mural for your classroom that will tell the story of Indiana.

1. Plan the scenes, from left to right, so the story will be told in the proper order.

2. Try to have all the children take part in the painting.

IV. Construct a scene. In the corner of the room or on a table construct a scene that shows some interesting event in Indiana history.

1. Build a trading post and fort with a stockade.

2. Build a pioneer home with the fireplace. Make some furniture.

3. Construct a mill, factory, mine, or store to show where many people work.

V. Plan ahead for an exhibit and a program. A display of objects brought in or constructed is a good review of work done. A program to which parents are invited can be fun.

1. Select the best art work, best stories, and poems to be arranged for an exhibit.

2. Show booklets, collections, posters, and scrapbooks.

3. Write the play yourselves. Select the scenes. Make the scenery and costumes. Choose the characters. Give the play for parents.

VI. Use Maps. Study outline maps and picture maps.

1. Use outline maps to locate rivers, cities, mountains, neighbor states, and to compare sizes and learn directions.

2. Draw from memory outline maps. Trace rivers and trails. Locate important places and events.

3. Construct picture maps to show products, famous buildings, and in-

teresting facts. Cut pictures from magazines and paste them in the proper places or draw small pictures and make a marginal key so that anyone can read the map.

4. Make floor maps. Draw a map on the floor or on heavy wrapping paper on the floor to learn directions and locations.

5. Learn to make salt and flour or paper pulp maps. The art teacher will help you.

Suggested Approaches

Teachers will need to build for themselves a broad background of information about the early history of Indiana and present day living in our state, in order to arouse and maintain the interest of children in the study of their home state.

Since many teachers will prefer to work out their own unique way of introducing the unit of work on Indiana, the following approaches are merely suggested.

1. MAPS—Display in the room a large wall map of Indiana, a map of the United States, another of the Northwest Territory, and any pictorial maps of Indiana that can be secured.

2. PICTURES AND POSTERS—Arrange on the bulletin board or section of the blackboard, pictures and posters that tell true stories of living in Indiana.

3. LIBRARY CORNER—The reading table and library corner should contain a collection of books, pamphlets, and leaflets that have pictures and information about Indiana. Storybooks on the elementary grade reading level should be included.

4. EXHIBIT—An arrangement of objects (coverlet, candle molds, spinning wheel, etc.) from pioneer homes, and various antiques may serve to arouse interest and questions concerning the early days in Indiana.

5. CONVERSATION AND DISCUSSION—A lively conversation and discussion of the following questions may be sufficient to introduce the unit to the group.

How well acquainted are you with your own state? Have you ever wondered how Indiana came to be the busy, comfortable place it is? Have people always had electric lights, telephones, and automobiles? How long have they enjoyed movies, airplanes, fast trains, and broadcasts from China, Russia, England, and Australia?